T0318616

Cambridge Elements

Elements in the Renaissance
edited by
John Henderson
Birkbeck, University of London, and Wolfson College, University of Cambridge
Jonathan K. Nelson
Syracuse University Florence

SENSES OF SPACE IN THE EARLY MODERN WORLD

Nicholas Terpstra
University of Toronto

CAMBRIDGE
UNIVERSITY PRESS

CAMBRIDGE
UNIVERSITY PRESS

Shaftesbury Road, Cambridge CB2 8EA, United Kingdom

One Liberty Plaza, 20th Floor, New York, NY 10006, USA

477 Williamstown Road, Port Melbourne, VIC 3207, Australia

314–321, 3rd Floor, Plot 3, Splendor Forum, Jasola District Centre,
New Delhi – 110025, India

103 Penang Road, #05–06/07, Visioncrest Commercial, Singapore 238467

Cambridge University Press is part of Cambridge University Press & Assessment,
a department of the University of Cambridge.

We share the University's mission to contribute to society through the pursuit of
education, learning and research at the highest international levels of excellence.

www.cambridge.org
Information on this title: www.cambridge.org/9781009462624

DOI: 10.1017/9781009435437

© Nicholas Terpstra 2024

First published 2024

A catalogue record for this publication is available from the British Library.

ISBN 978-1-009-46262-4 Hardback
ISBN 978-1-009-43540-6 Paperback
ISSN 2631-9101 (online)
ISSN 2631-9098 (print)

Senses of Space in the Early Modern World

Elements in the Renaissance

DOI: 10.1017/9781009435437
First published online: February 2024

Nicholas Terpstra
University of Toronto

Author for correspondence: Nicholas Terpstra, nicholas.terpstra@utoronto.ca

Abstract: How did early moderns experience sense and space? How did the expanding cultural, political, and social horizons of the period emerge out of those experiences and further shape them? This Element takes an approach that is both globally expansive and locally rooted by focusing on four cities as key examples: Florence, Amsterdam, Boston, and Manila. They relate to distinct parts of European cultural and colonialist experience from north to south, republican to monarchical, Catholic to Protestant. Without attempting a comprehensive treatment, the Element aims to convey the range of distinct experiences of space and sense as these varied by age, gender, race, and class. Readers see how sensory and spatial experiences emerged through religious cultures that were themselves shaped by temporal rhythms, and how sound and movement expressed gathering economic and political forces in an emerging global order. This title is also available as Open Access on Cambridge Core.

Keywords: spatial history, history of the senses, early modern history, urban history, global history

ISBNs: 9781009462624 (HB), 9781009435406 (PB), 9781009435437 (OC)
ISSNs: 2631-9101 (online), 2631-9098 (print)

Contents

1 Thinking with Space and Sense

1.1 When and Why?

How did early moderns experience sense and space? How did the expanding cultural, political, and social horizons of the period emerge out of those experiences and further shape them? The period 1400–1750 was when ideas about the world and experiences of it were changing rapidly. Intellectual and religious movements challenged traditional ideas about the universe, humanity, and God. Artists and writers experimented with more naturalistic ways of conveying their own experiences and visions. Global networks were realigning as merchants and explorers began moving in larger circuits on land and water, sometimes spending months or even years on voyages whose direction and outcome were often uncertain. Europeans in particular were searching out engagements with cultures distant from them in time and space – ancient Greece and Rome were prominent on their aspirational horizons while Asia, Africa, and the Americas came to define their physical horizons. Europeans initially came with curiosity and sometimes a sense of awe, particularly when encountering the courts in Istanbul, Beijing, Delhi, and Tenochtitlan. Awe would turn to opportunity, and they would soon be seeking ways to possess, control, and profit from a world that they increasingly came to think of as *theirs*.

This early modern shift from awe to opportunity generated modern Europe's most profound global impacts: nation-states, capitalism, colonialism, racism, and environmental change. Yet it would take the length of those centuries for Europeans to realize their dominance. Many of those whom Europeans encountered were more bemused than threatened by their ambitions. The Ottomans, Mughals, and Ming Chinese were all wealthier, militarily stronger, and culturally more advanced than Europeans and would remain so till the end of the period. In Asia, Europeans were kept on a short leash by the Chinese and Japanese, restricted to small numbers in controlled settlements and subject to expulsion. Beyond the coastal forts from which they traded in enslaved peoples, Europeans made little impact on Africa. In much of the Americas, they depended on Indigenous nations and survived largely through alliances with them. It was in the Americas that they would have the largest impact, due as much to diseases like smallpox that they brought with them as to their efforts to dominate Indigenous groups. None of this is meant to deny that Europeans of the early modern period could be ruthless, exclusionary, and convinced of their own superiority. We just shouldn't be too quick to take their word for it. The early modern period is when these ambitions moved in fits and starts from rhetoric to reality and when Europeans' movement from dependence to domination generated ever more profound effects on people and the environment across the globe.

This is not a study of the economics and politics of early modern globalization. I'm aiming instead to explore how that process shaped the ways that people in different parts of the world inhabited spaces, and how their senses may have picked up these and other changes. Can we recreate how early moderns saw? What they smelled and, more to the point, what smells meant to them? Were they anxious about touch? Did they measure with sound or with smell? Can we understand how they registered or responded to any of these emotionally? Some historians think that early modern senses and emotion are largely inaccessible to us (Boddick and Smith 2020). Their skepticism is understandable. Senses are historical, and we shouldn't underestimate how distant and foreign they are (Smith 2021). We rely heavily on what people in the past wrote, but we'd be fooling ourselves to imagine that a handful of texts by the few people who could and did write could allow us to recreate how people in the past – any past – *really* saw, experienced, tasted, or felt. But skepticism needn't stop there. If we read their philosophical or religious texts, we're no more certain that we *really* understand the thoughts and beliefs that early moderns were writing about. The same is true of diplomatic correspondence, diaries, or parliamentary debates used to understand political history. If our goal is to understand the past as it actually happened, we'll inevitably be frustrated by the limits of our sources and the disconnections in time. And that's *before* considering the paradoxes, contradictions, uncertainties, and deceptions of those we're studying. History is a conversation between past and present. Whether we're creating a Renaissance video game, writing a historical novel, or researching a scholarly monograph, the history we produce is always in part about ourselves. It requires us to be conscious and self-aware, aiming as much as possible to keep from turning our historical subjects into personal objects. We can't presume to know completely what Shakespeare felt, any more than we really know what Machiavelli thought. Yet to imagine that they are completely foreign to us, or that feelings are inherently less accessible than thoughts, is to adopt an abstract standard of historical knowledge that's ultimately self-defeating.

One way to work all this out is to approach senses in relation to each other and to other experiences. A wealth of recent work allows us to guess how sense and space intersected in ways we're no longer familiar with. Early moderns were alert to the biological impact of noises. They thought that some forms of sight involved eyes and objects touching each other. They measured time by not only hands on clocks but also tastes and sounds. Smells that were strange or familiar were recalibrating their sense of order. Sometimes it's more important to read their silences than their words. I'll aim to foreground experiences and will only occasionally detour to give a quick idea of some theories that early moderns relied on to explain how senses *worked*. I hope this takes us some way to moving beyond the pages of manuscripts and books and into what's been described as the *sensorium*, the often unwritten and unspoken context for the documents we're more accustomed to dealing with.

1.2 Sites

I'll take an approach that is both globally expansive and locally rooted by returning periodically to four cities for some key examples: Florence, Amsterdam, Boston, and Manila. Without attempting a comprehensive treatment, I'll use these places to convey something of the *range* of distinct experiences of space and sense, showing as much as possible how these varied by age, gender, race, and class.

Why these four cities? They allow us to take a sounding of early modern experiences of sense and space that is comparative and interdisciplinary. We have an older south European city, Florence, with a stable population that reconstructs traditional and classical forms to meet new political realities. A north European commercial city, Amsterdam, was rapidly erecting new neighborhoods and buildings that reflected global capitalist and colonialist links while accommodating a large influx of migrants from distinct religious and racial communities across Europe. Both cities demonstrate the emerging phenomenon of the capital city – Florence the literal capital of a newly expanded territorial state and Amsterdam the virtual capital of a fast-expanding commercial empire. These European cities will be compared to two port cities founded as European colonial entrepôts. Manila was built by the Spanish on the site of an ancient conquered settlement, Maynilad, that had long been a hub for regional trade. Boston was founded by English settlers where Indigenous peoples had gathered over centuries for meetings and trade. Both were the colonial outposts of quite distinct national political regimes and religious cultures. Yet both also had a sometimes distant and conflicted relationship with those regimes and cultures. Both gained their structure and character from immediate and intense interactions with local Indigenous peoples and through land and seaborne trading networks that extended out into their broader regions.

Each of these four cities possesses rich historiographical mines of material on both spatial and sensory experience. Florence and Amsterdam pivot between classical and modern traditions – both used the classical inheritance that the Renaissance period valued in order to legitimate social, political, and cultural innovations. Manila and Boston emerged in quite different colonial contexts but demonstrated strong parallels in Europeans' relations to both Indigenous and enslaved peoples and the natural environment. Looking at all four cities also allows us to engage with different sides of the early modern capitalist and colonial experience. They relate to distinct parts of the European cultural tradition from north to south, from republican to monarchical, from Catholic to Protestant. Other cities and towns will certainly come into the narrative, as will rural areas both in themselves and in relation to urban life. Yet I'll return to these four regularly in order to plot parallels and demonstrate continuities as we move through the experiences of space and sense. In this way we'll be able to explore how sensory and spatial experiences emerged through cultures and exchanges that were themselves shaped by temporal rhythms. We'll see how sight, sound, smell, taste, and touch may help us understand some impacts of economic and political forces.

1.3 Approaches and Intersections

Different authors have written about space and the sensorium, and the most revealing approaches look at space and the senses in relation to each other rather than separately. Two French authors have been particularly critical for helping us think of how space is something that we don't simply receive, encounter, or occupy. It is produced by our actions and use of it. Henri Lefevre's *The Production of Space* and Michel de Certeau's *The Practice of Everyday Life* launched the field by probing how space and sense intersect and how our experience of them lies in that very interaction, and not simply in perception of something objectively "there." Lefevre described this as *lived space* and de Certeau termed it *space as a practiced place* (de Certeau 1984; Lefevre 1991). How did early moderns' social and political relations create space, and how did that creation and experience evolve from childhood into old age? How did gender and race raise new social and cultural barriers to channel experience at different ages? Beyond this lens of intersectionality, historians have more recently grappled with how to capture exchange and conflict within spaces. Mobility inevitably becomes critical to how space is practiced. De Certeau aimed to break the hold of two-dimensional maps and recover the city of well-traveled streets and empty squares, periodic markets, and fixed taverns, frequently visited churches and shrines, and frequently avoided courts and prisons. Locals and visitors would create a city by foot that was more personal and sensory than the map they might hold in their hand. These spaces were relational and defined even in official documents by who lived here and who worked there; this was what Nicholas Eckstein described as the "prepositional city" where we locate a house by its neighbors on either side and the nearby corner rather than by a number (Eckstein 2018). But more than a building, we locate the house as a group of residents known by their relations with neighbors and the moving life of the street. Mobility can bring conflict, particularly in colonial settings where colonizers and colonized, enslaved and indentured, settled and new arrivals all face off and compete. Mary Louise Pratt described these asymmetrical places where cultures clash as "contact zones" marked by conflict (Pratt 2008), while Cécile Fromont has expanded the discussion beyond conflicts by addressing the movement of many people into and through "spaces of correlation" like Nkumba a Ngudi (also known as São Salvadore) in the Kingdom of Kongo. These spaces are characterized by various forms of reciprocity, engagement, and sharing, and are best expressed with the French word *éspaces*. They are where individuals and groups take up "ideas and forms belonging to radically different realms, confront them, and eventually turn them into interrelated parts of a new system of thought and expression" (Fromont 2014, 15).

These distinct approaches share a common desire to bring mobility, migration, and lived experience into our understanding of early modern spaces. Returning to de Certeau, sight, sound, smell, taste, and touch are vital to the practice that turns place into space. The senses invest physical places with emotion and become the referents that define our memories of spaces and turn them into what Pierre Nora described as resonant "sites of memory" (*lieux de memoire* – Nora 1989, 1998). Some authors have used artistic, cultural, and sensory expression to push thinking about space beyond physical extension alone. Musicologist R. Murray Schafer developed the idea of the "soundscape" as a means of capturing the merging of sound and memory, as both an environment in particular places and an individual experience (Schafer 1977). J. Douglas Porteus adapted this in his idea of the "smellscape," where again the olfactory environment incorporated not only the smells registered immediately in a particular place but also the memories and past experiences associated with it (Porteous 1985; Xiao, Tate, and Kang 2018; Lindborg and Liew 2021). With this the game was on, and more recent adaptations have been a bit opportunistic: the idea of "tastescapes" hasn't been widely developed outside of culinary contexts and tour guides, while "touchscape" has been used to describe both touch-sensitive software and the methods of maintaining inner balance and mindfulness (Kabat-Zinn 2013). In some cases, the connections are more to cultural fields than to physical spaces. After "soundscapes" and "smellscapes" worked their way into the language, anthropologist Arjun Appadurai began writing of "ethnoscapes," "mediascapes," "technoscapes," "financescapes," and "ideoscapes" as the cultural dimensions of modern globalization. Medievalist Guy Geltner anatomized "healthscaping." All reflected both political and social positions and the "constructed landscape of collective aspirations" (Appadurai 1996, 31–3; Klaver 2014; Geltner 2019).

Appadurai was bringing together both the social reality that situates people and the imaginative process that make their position a reflection of aspirations about space rather than just a sensing of stimuli. We're back to the skepticism noted earlier – one reason we can't fully understand the senses of the past is because we have difficulty capturing what early moderns were imagining and hoping for when they saw, heard, smelled, tasted, or touched (Smith 2007). And yet. Schafer began the process by building on the idea of landscape painting, and returning there may help us move forward. In the booming art market of seventeenth-century Netherlands, landscapes made up perhaps half of all paintings sold. They were the most popular genre by far in a culture where artisans, recently arrived migrants, refugees, and even relatively poor people were all buying canvases (Chong 1987). The Netherlands was among the most intensely urbanized regions of Europe, and Irene Klaver highlights why city dwellers hung these idealized rural spaces on their wall. "More than depicting the 'real' situation of the region or landscape around them, the early painters reflected what people were expecting or wanting to see: the painted landscape documents form an indication of early Dutch social imaginary, its identity in its cultural perception and reception of the changes in their landscape" (Klaver 2014, 4). Simon Schama suggests that imagined landscapes were "a way of looking; of rediscovering what we already have, but which somehow eludes our recognition and our appreciation. Instead of being yet another explanation of what we have lost, it is an exploration of what we may yet find" (Schama 1995, 14). The shoemaker who put up a landscape wasn't just seeking the outdoors; the landscape he hung was often of imagined dunes and wild spaces that he longed to inhabit, and not familiar farm fields crisscrossed with grids of canals and roads.

R. Murray Schafer had in mind precisely this intersection of urban and rural, manufactured and natural, real and aspirational sounds when developing the idea of the "soundscape." He aimed to capture environmental sound in critique of the erasure of natural sounds like bird calls through the layering of urban noise pollution (Schafer 1977). Theatre historian Bruce R. Smith compared urban and rural soundscapes and speculated on the relative decibel levels each experienced in daily life. He defined the "acoustic horizon" of how far voices, bells, and bird calls might travel in open city streets, enclosed theatres, or across country fields. Like Schama and Klaver, Smith extended this to the early modern imaginary by noting how Baroque composers sought to echo these bird calls and other natural sounds in their music as a means of expressing the ideal and potentially purifying power of nature (Smith 1999). Niall Atkinson further connects perception, regulation, and aspiration in sound. He describes how Florentines used bells to regulate and pace urban life as their "sonic armature" before moving on to show how a broadly distributed and acute sense of the officially regulated sequence of bells turned any disruption of that routine into a siren call. This was precisely how laborers summoned each other when launching a social revolt in 1378 (Atkinson 2016). Sound constitutes groups and shapes their practice of place: Tess Knighton has developed Barry Truax' concept of "acoustic communities," which she describes as "any soundscape in which acoustic information plays a pervasive role in the lives of the inhabitants." Gangs, confraternities, the enslaved, refugees, and performers all used shared sounds to organize themselves, communicate, and distinguish themselves from those around them. For Knighton, the significant role of sound lies in the perception that "acoustic cues and signals constantly keep the community in touch with what is going on from day-to-day within it" (Truax 2016, 253; Champion 2017; Knighton 2018).

Understanding *land*scapes, *sound*scapes, and *smell*scapes as all in part constructed, imagined, and aspirational helps us to see that sensescapes were *e*scapes as much as anything else. Early moderns weren't only receiving stimuli but were also using them to construct their understandings, hopes, and anxieties about the world. They were doing this at a time when intellectual and geographical horizons were rapidly expanding. How they braided sense, place, and emotion gives us a better idea of their experience of the world and their mentality in it. In order to convey this, I'll connect different senses and spaces, opening with how spaces looked and operated, moving then to sound as a force, exploring how smells were located in sites both physical and personal, noting how taste might be used to set or mark time, and then closing with ideas of when and how people were to use touch. I'm not aiming to offer a systematic survey or a detailed review of those senses that were most typical or significant, but will highlight intersections of senses and space that were indicative, new, and compelling. I'll focus on some that may seem marginal in the hope of using the unexpected or unfamiliar to remind us how differently the people in this period sensed the world and occupied it. While it's common to think that early moderns were moving to a stronger sense of themselves as individuals, in many cases they were far more preoccupied with each other. Producing space as a sensorium was something you did in community, and so much of what we'll look at will be collective, communal, and shared.

2 The Sight of Space

Early modern cities unfolded around a series of open and closed spaces. Roads and squares set the basic pattern of the urban fabric and directed people around markets, shops, churches, and homes. People animated these spaces as they used and moved through them, and since most were walking, these public spaces were where life happened. Artisans carried work out into the streets for light, sales, and sociability. Squares were jammed with stalls on some days and empty on others. Thoroughfares first laid down by the ancient Romans continued to carry the bulk of traffic through some towns. They drew straight lines between gates laid out like compass points, though often with unexpected detours – a curve marked where the road exited a wall demolished centuries before or bent around a church that commemorated a miracle. Water, hills, and marsh set the basic landscape that shaped the layout of every urban fabric. Port cities might bend and curve over hills rising from the seashore like Boston's compact Shawmut Peninsula, or be built around river deltas like Manila, or build their own topography of canals channeling water through blocks firmed up by sunken piles and bounded by stone walls like Amsterdam. The Roman soldiers who had laid out Florence set it apart from and at an angle to the Arno River – a grid pattern still clear in modern maps – but Florentines embraced and bridged the temperamental river. In Manila the intersections of different cultures were written on the landscape itself: one settlement laid out in a grid and set behind walls like a Roman camp, others clustered more organic-ally on either side of the Pasig River, and yet others stretched out along the arc of Manila Bay. Any settlement built on a river or shore repeatedly fell victim to floods or storms, but that water shaped city spaces and life. Water was the first elemental horizon setting the sight of space.

2.1 Open and Closed

City life pushed inland from ports and wharves, and most of those doing the pushing were men: soldiers, sailors, packers, and shippers navigated the space with mixed languages that spoke to long travels and lives of constant negotiation. These "spaces of arrival" defined ports like Amsterdam, Manila, and Venice and fed a capillary network of warehouses, shops, and dormitories diffusing inland (Salzburg 2018). Arrivals to smaller ports and riverine cities might be through gates rather than on wharves, but buildings on adjoining streets and squares served the same purpose. Women were more evident in the taverns and hostels offering rest, food, and entertainment as proprietors, servants, and sex workers. These were contact zones where residents and migrants met. Most were warrens of warehouses and wharves that effectively walled off the port, with impressive customs houses and a few trading shops providing liminal access points where power, authority, and money were exchanged. Some of those arriving by boat never passed into the city, and some in the city seldom went to the port. It wasn't just geography: gender, age, class, race, and status determined who could cross over the invisible boundary and how.

Each of these cities that opened to a port on one side also sheltered behind a wall on the other. Wall and water defined the urban space. All the cities we're focusing on here had walls, though among them Boston's were the least impressive. The wooden stockade that crossed the narrow neck joining its peninsula to the mainland was little more than a suggestion and better for keeping out animals than anything or anyone else. But Bostonians held to it for a century and a half – it had a gate, customs collectors, moat, guards, and cannons. Together with batteries on outlying islands it made the city a fortress (see Figure 1). The wall would be rebuilt in stone and brick and wasn't completely demolished until 1822 (Peterson 2019). More than defense, it marked where Bostonians thought that urban space began. Florentines had been in the business of building walls far longer with major concentric circuits of 1078, 1173–5, and 1284. The steady growth of their economy and ambitions through expanding trade to the Levant, northern Europe, and Italy itself led them to erect a final set by 1333, but the Black Death collapsed Florence's population little more than a dozen years later. As in cities around Europe, a plague that swept a third, a half, or more of the urban population into the

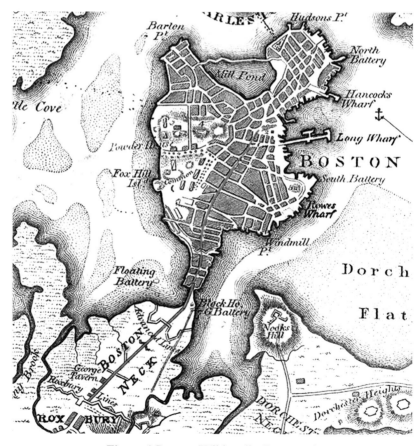

Figure 1 Boston (Wikimedia Commons)

grave left large stretches of open space within the last circuit of walls. Farms, tenements for poor workers, and a jumble of separate enclosures for nuns, monks, orphans, the sick, the dying, and beggars filled the gap. Amsterdammers defended their settlement with new sets of walls and moats from 1340, 1385, 1482, and 1515, their circuits traceable to this day on streets and canals bearing the descriptive names "front citywall/voorburgwal" and "back citywall/achterburg-wal." New fortunes and fears of Spanish and French invaders led Amsterdam to build new walls in 1585 and 1613 before launching the most ambitious circuit in 1657–63. This final circuit extended for many kilometers and was built on thousands of piles sunk deep into the sandy soil (Abrahamse 2019).

These sets of city walls all aimed to incorporate and defend entire urban populations and to demonstrate in brick and stone where city life started – or ended: Boston, Florence, and Amsterdam each built large permanent gallows outside a key city gate to underscore the terms of admission to urban community. Those for Amsterdam were located where sailors could see them as they entered the port and were large enough to hold over a dozen bodies at a time (Gobin 2021). Manila's walls deliberately kept most of the settlement's residents out. A walled compound known as *Intramuros* separated and isolated Spanish colonists from the far larger Chinese and Japanese settlements located outside the walls and across the Pasig River and also from the Tagalog villages known as *arrabales* extending along the bay. Manila's first wooden walls had sheltered all these populations from assault by land or sea, but as stone walls were erected the protected space was reserved for Spaniards and their households. These Spanish settlers were not alone in making walls the visible marker of separate spaces for distinct cultural and ethnic groups: Japanese and Chinese authorities channeled foreign traders into similar compounds in Nagasaki and Macao, the Ottomans had long done the same with migrants to Istanbul, Salonika, and Izmir, Indigenous communities camped outside the stockades of Boston, Quebec, and Montreal, and Hanseatic merchants trading in London sailed to wharves in a walled complex known as the Steelyard.

This dynamic of open and closed spaces defined the roads and squares of early modern cities. We often forget the sheer number and variety of closed spaces. However porous the walls of one or another might be – more so for merchants, less so for nuns – enclosures of different sorts were critical regulators of urban space and life. They defined who could move where and when, and even whether they could move at all. Enclosures gave built form to a host of social boundaries around age, gender, status, and religion that have largely disappeared from most of these cities. As we move from port, wharf, and gate further into these cities and aim to recover the sight of urban space and understand its connection to social life, we need to recover these jumbled lengths of walls. We need to see who they enclosed and why and when.

In the seventh century, as the cities built by the ancient Romans were disintegrating, Spanish bishop Isidore of Seville wrote that "a city, *civitas,* is a multitude of people united by a bond of fellowship . . . *Urbs* is the town itself, the *civitas* is not rocks, but the inhabitants" (Rubin 2020, 9). While the walls of Florence and Amsterdam and even Boston's stumpy stockade merged the cities of buildings (*urbs*) and of people (*civitas*), Manila's *Intramuros* became distinctly early modern and colonial in dividing them. As if to underscore that life outside the enclosure was perilous, Spanish authorities fostered tensions between Chinese, Japanese, and Tagalog communities outside the walls and triggered or abetted intercommunal riots that killed thousands: possibly 20,000 Chinese died in each of the explosions of 1603 and 1639 alone, with more following in 1686 and 1762 (Tremml-Warner 2015; Reyes 2017).

Early moderns multiplied the walls that segregated and distinguished groups, as we see on the roads that stretch in from city gates. Entering Florence's main northern gate of San Gallo puts us on the street of the same name (see Figure 2). It

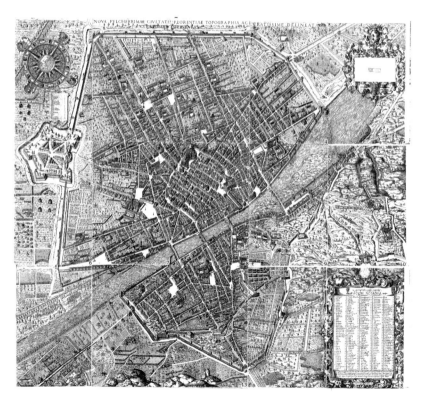

Figure 2 Florence. Stefano Buonsignori, 1584 (Harvard Map Collection, Harvard Library)

is the extension of the ancient Roman *cardo*, the north–south axis that continues over the famous shop-lined bridge (Ponte Vecchio) that for centuries gave the only passage across the Arno River and then on out the city's main southern gate, the Porta Romana. Lost gates at each of the city's former circuits of walls act as prisms refracting the street's route, but it funneled all travelers arriving from northern Europe and heading on to Rome. Outside San Gallo at the north lay a cluster of hostels and warehouses, including one to quarantine goods in times of plague – early moderns were convinced that textiles could harbor plague. Walking through the gate didn't bring you directly into the bustle of an international entrepôt, but to a series of blank walled enclosures. Convents lined this stretch of road, alternating with enclosures for those who weren't nuns or monks: the Broccardi hostel for pilgrims, which from the 1540s housed orphaned boys and poor men; the Messer Bonifazio infirmary next door to it; and the S. Trinità syphilitics' hospital just down the street. These walls were less forbidding, and while the Broccardi had a portico, all gates were locked. The road continued past the ghetto, which from 1571 enclosed Tuscany's Jewish community in a city block whose jumbled warrens had housed Florence's main brothel for a century and a half before. San Gallo's enclosures alternated with open spaces like the huge open market adjoining the ghetto, the piazza of San Lorenzo kitty-corner from the palace built by the merchant Medici in the fifteenth century, and the enormous square fronting the ducal palace they erected across the Arno in the next century. Walking San Gallo brought you past a series of open and closed spaces, each setting the other off, the open ones thronging with those locked out of the closed.

Fewer enclosures marked the street south of the Arno, but across the city dozens of enclosures filled vacant plots just inside the walls: more convents and monasteries, a workhouse for beggars to the southwest, shelters for abandoned adolescent girls to the northwest and northeast. Most were built in the fifteenth and sixteenth centuries. Similar convents and enclosures marked the grid of streets inside Manila's *Intramuros* (see Figure 3): by the mid-eighteenth century there were eight religious houses, five residential schools, and two hospitals, all segregated by gender, caste, and race (Graham 2019). In Amsterdam they are in the core of the city, where many occupy former convents or monasteries closed when Catholicism was outlawed in 1578. City fathers installed orphans of middle-ranked families in the former St. Lucien cloister (*Burgerweeshuis* or Citizen Orphanage) from 1580, sent young men needing correction to the former convent of Poor Clares from 1596 (*Rasphuis* or Workhouse), and in 1663–5 built a new home for poorer orphans (*Aalmoezeniersweeshuis* or Almoners' Orphanage) that soon housed 1,300 (McCants 1997, Abrahamse 2019).

Walking the city streets brought this alternation of open and closed spaces, of bustling and sometimes chaotic market spaces jammed with traders, food

Figure 3 Manila. Pedro Murillo Velarde, 1734 (Wikimedia Commons)

sellers, town criers, and people watching the view, set off by windowless walls sealing out sight and, less effectively, sound from those locked inside. Each required the other. Charitable enclosures bordering squares and lining streets were opened and driven by a mix of motives: were the poor genuinely needy or just deviant? With migrants pouring into cities from all quarters, city leaders invoked God and took fatherly authority and care over everyone, much as they did in their own homes and families. Large public buildings were as much the calling card for powerful and beneficent governments as big open markets. Impressive and increasingly impregnable charitable enclosures merged *urbs* and *civitas* visually and spatially at the most strategic intersections. Amsterdam's Citizen Orphanage overlooked the boundary canal of the Spui and its new Almoners' Orphanage stretched its facade across a full city block in its newest residential district. London's Bridewell Palace on the Thames River was built as Henry VIII's main city residence in the 1520s, became an enclosed orphanage in the 1550s, and by the end of the century was a prison. From 1652 Genoa's Beggars' Workhouse (Albergo dei Poveri) began the expansion that would within decades leave it looming on the hills above the city (further expansions 1667, 1689, 1702). Ironically, when French warships turned their cannons on the city in a siege of 1684, Genoa's city fathers took shelter in this palatial enclosure they'd built to imprison beggars.

2.2 Space as Place

The men and women running the enclosed houses and hospitals in Amsterdam, London, Manila, and elsewhere positioned themselves as surrogate fathers and mothers offering protective shelter and parental direction to orphaned, abandoned, or delinquent children and youths. We should remember that only a fraction of such children were institutionalized in this way. Most joined more informal networks of "child circulation" involving neighbors, extended family, guilds, or confraternities (Harrington 2009). But early moderns prided themselves on this expanding institutionalization and used more than enclosures to make it visible. On those rare and regulated times when young wards left the homes to work, raise alms, or collect gifts of food, they wore uniforms that made their enclosures as immediate and visible as a wall. Blue or red smocks, distinctive badges, and colored hats took their shelter identity out onto streets far beyond the home itself, publicly marked and categorized by their clothes (Presciutti 2023).

But who did not walk the streets in uniform? Every government set troops on the streets for daytime protection and night watch. On the rare times that nuns left their enclosures, the cut and color of their habits and veils advertised those same convents. The friars staffing Manila's male religious houses wore habits that even a child could identify as Franciscan, Augustinian, Jesuit, or Dominican. And not only Christian children: to prevent disputes between missionaries, Spanish officials assigned particular orders to one or other of the communities outside the *Intramuros*. Dominicans worked among the Chinese *sangleyes* community called the *parian* upstream from the *Intramuros*, Franciscans among the Japanese settled across the Pasig River in Dilao, and Jesuits among the Tagalog across the Luzon peninsula. They built schools to plant faith among children and harvest it across families. The strategy brought them more converts in neighborhoods where children lived than in the less domestically rooted migrant communities of largely male Japanese and Chinese merchants and artisans (Tremml-Warner 2015). The cut and color of uniforms extended the spaces of a city's enclosures in a reminder of the diversity of its *civitas*.

Living in the *civitas* made you an insider only if you were part of a community that could mobilize space. Groups of Florentine artisans and day laborers gathered in *potenze* that elected kings and courts to organize festive neighborhood street parties and demonstrations that supported or opposed the Medici rulers. They marked their territory with small stone plaques embedded in the walls at intersections, following a local tradition that families like the Medici and institutions like hospitals had long adopted to brand space.

Marching up and down these same streets with banners, robes, and dozens of members, confraternities took mobile possession of their neighborhoods, imitating rural confraternities that "beat the bounds" by walking the perimeter of *their* territory. Manilans enjoyed dressing up with silks, ribbons, hats, and fine shoes for the daily *paseo* in the late afternoon. Amsterdam's night watches sent groups of urban merchants patrolling dark streets after curfew. Defense, sociability, territoriality, and ritual merged and these groups of men spun webs of civic networks when processing and patrolling streets and squares, determining who might walk where and when. They were taking possession of the space – much of this was the motion of insiders who were turning space into place as they turned corners and walked the lengths of streets, stopping to talk with neighbors, eat with friends, and pray to God (Rosenthal 2015; Reyes 2017; Rombough 2024).

If these were insiders, who was outside? It's one thing to distinguish inside and outside of walls and enclosures. Authorities might aim to merge spatial and social distinctions, but these purely legal walls had ways of cracking and falling apart. The 2,400 Spanish and mestizos living within Manila's Intramuros in 1620 were certainly inside, but were the 20,000 Tagalog, 26,000 Chinese, and 5,000 Japanese really "outsiders"? Getting accurate numbers is almost impossible: in 1621 there were 21,000 licensed Chinese paying a poll tax and an estimated 5,000 unlicensed. These merchants and artisans did more to turn Manila into a global entrepôt with wharves, warehouses, and workshops lined up and down the Pasig river than a handful of Spanish soldiers, clergy, and administrators holed up behind their stone walls (Herzog 2003; Tremml-Warner 2015; Graham 2019). Yet distrust, fear, and prejudice marked relations with the Chinese in particular, with violent riots and expulsions in 1603, 1639, 1662, 1686, and 1762. The riot of 1603, supported by the local Tagalog, may have claimed 25,000 lives, while that of 1639 may have claimed a further 22–24,000. The Spanish were more welcoming to the Japanese when aiming to enter Japan themselves, though riots broke out 1605–9, and relations declined after the Japanese restricted access to Nagasaki in 1624 and 1638 (Reyes 2017). At the other end of the spectrum, Amsterdam sucked in merchants and laborers from across Northern Europe, while Florence had for centuries drawn from the whole Tuscan territory and beyond. In both cities the wealthier and more ambitious marked their arrivals with impressive structures. Some of these were forced migrants: Amsterdam drew in many Protestant refugees when Spanish troops sacked Antwerp in 1576 and again when pogroms erupting in the Polish Lithuanian commonwealth in 1648 sent Jews fleeing for their lives (Teller 2020).

The insider/outsider binary breaks down on the streets of these cities, and the experience of Europe's Jews highlights that. The early modern period was when the drives to expel or enclose them were at their peak. Religious and political authorities argued whether urban spaces could bear the sight of them, and accelerating expulsions from cities in Germany, France, and Italy through the fifteenth century peaked with the mass evictions of the continent's largest communities from Spain (1492) and Portugal (1497). Jewish families stretched across Europe with confusing contradictions of inside and outside, insider and outsider. The ghetto that Florence opened in 1571 mirrored those built in Venice (1516) and Rome (1555). Were the ninety-seven recorded in a 1567 census of the Jews part of the Florentine *civitas*? Or the 200 forcibly relocated there from across northern Tuscany in 1571? Or the 600 living there five generations later in 1680? Like nuns, prostitutes, and orphans, they too walked the city's streets with signs that turned their clothes into uniforms advertising their spatial and racial enclosure: yellow or red circles, hats, bells, or badges. Their signs and rights were continually renegotiated with authorities who added or suspended terms at will. The terms were contractually guaranteed, with all the permanence that a sheet of paper affords (Siegmund 2006; Cassen 2017; Katz 2017; Walden 2019). Walking and working locally made them part of the Florentine *civitas* but never Florentine citizens.

Jewish communities in Prague and Hamburg were just as spatially segregated, though without walls. Those earning a living in Strasbourg were forced to live outside the city entirely, entering by day and exiting by nightfall. Amsterdam toyed with the idea of a Jewish district before backing gradually into a more open spatial coexistence that turned it into a portal for the descendants of forcibly baptized Iberian Jews aiming to recover their ancestral faith (Kaplan 2000; Abrahamse 2019). Venice's Jews hired local carpenters to fit synagogues into existing buildings of the ghetto, and when Prague's Jews had started their synagogue in 1274 they dug deep below street level to keep it discreetly out of a skyline defined by church steeples. Amsterdam's Jewish community sank piles into the mud and raised the walls of two monumental synagogues built in a distinctly local style for steadily growing numbers of Sephardic and Ashkenazic migrants who moved into homes spread through surrounding neighborhoods. One moved further: the first Jew recorded in Boston, Solomon Franco, was a Sephardic Jew who arrived from the Netherlands in 1649 as an agent for a Dutch merchant and was ordered to leave within weeks. Five years later a group of twenty-three Sephardic Jews fleeing Recife after the Portuguese reconquered Brazil from the Dutch arrived in New Amsterdam. Governor Pieter Stuyvesant was set to expel them until his employers in the Amsterdam-based Dutch West India Company pointed out that expulsion would be unreasonable and unfair. Not to mention impolitic, since some held shares in the unprofitable Company itself. The group gained permission to remain and open a burial ground, but it would be decades before they could establish a synagogue (Hertzberg 1991).

The Jews of Venice, Rome, Prague, Amsterdam, and New Amsterdam all had spaces in their cities, but were these places? They had to be careful how they were seen in them. Be too much in the eye and you might be thrown out the gate. But outside the gate there might be many others who made life inside possible. The more we tally the number of migrant and marginal groups in and around any city, the more the distinction of insider and outsider breaks down – as it long had (Rubin, 2020). Asking whether the Chinese were part of Manila is laughable, and the Tagalog even more so. As we move to the eighteenth century, it was left to words to reinforce and raise new walls, like the theories of race that evoked biology and the legal restraints that punished intermarriage.

2.3 Imagined Spaces

All roads may not have led to the center, but all traffic certainly did. Joining the flow of those walking down streets, particularly in some parade or procession, inevitably brought you to a space where the sight lines opened up and pulled your eyes up with them. The steeple on Boston's Christ Church was the city's tallest structure. The bell tower of Florence's seat of civic government vied for height with the bell tower beside its nearby cavernous cathedral crowned with the famous dome that could, in Michelangelo's view, shelter all of Tuscany (Atkinson 2016). Italians cited bell towers when calling out localist obsessions – *campanilismo* or "tower pride." A forest of spires and towers greeted those sailing into Amsterdam, as indeed it would greet anyone coming by foot into almost any town in Europe. In 1544 Sebastian Munster published *Cosmografia*, an illustrated atlas of maps and city views whose wild success – twenty-four Latin editions over the next century – signaled a popular visual obsession with urban space and place. A troupe of mapmakers and engravers fed the booming market for illustrated atlases containing aerial views and skylines of cities with distinctive towers punctuating the streets and squares inside circuits of walls, while improbably bare and empty rural spaces lay outside them. In 1572 Georg Braun and Franz Hogenberg published the first edition of *Cities of the World* (*Civitates Orbis Terrarum*), which over the next four decades grew to six volumes identifying the walls, towers, squares, and streets of 546 cities around the world (see Figure 4). The sight of a tower identified and inspired, but its sound was a call to action. Towers without bells were mute and so quite literally were almost unheard of. Instead, most towns packed big bells and small into

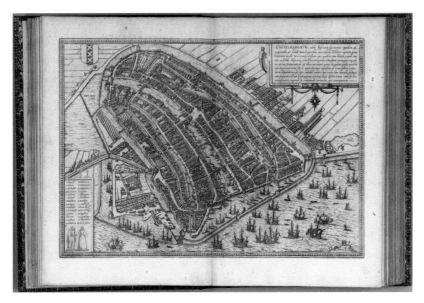

Figure 4 Amsterdam. G. Braun and F. Hogenberg, 1575 (David Rumsey Map Collection)

their towers and developed a language of peals and calls that opened the town's markets, workplaces, and offices in the morning, closed them at night, and summoned city dwellers in times of crisis. But more on them below.

Manila was rare in not having a spire to lift eyes far above the expansive bulk of its cathedral, though it did have a tower filled with bells. And the space they filled extended out sonically and visually. The Spanish perfected the urbanistic form of the central square – the Plaza Major – where a vast open space was framed with solid stone buildings where authority was exercised: church, governor's palace, town hall, court, guild hall. How do you transmit the abstractions of power? The promises of heaven and threats of hell, the constitutions of officials and commands of rulers, the obligations of contracts – all of these moved from texts and treatises into tactile and terrestrial form in the buildings that ringed the central square. You saw and heard power. Peals of bells opened courts, closed markets, called Christians to worship or announced Christ's clockwork arrival when a priest consecrated the host in the mass (Atkinson 2016). Processions of rulers, troops, or spiritual celebrants moved out from these buildings to animate and occupy neighborhoods. But the processions always returned. Like the diminishing resonances of bells, they brought attention back to the square or structure where power was seated. The physical seat was a proxy for something greater: an elaborate courthouse pointed to justice; a governor's palace embodied royal authority; and a council hall expressed a charter or constitution. All included archives where stacks of paper put social relations in black and white as a means of defying time and fixing memory. A church was the eternal God's concession to temporality. Buildings were metaphors that the imagination filled out, and this was why they had to be so visual, tactile, and sensorily resonant. Building a public hall, church, or square was an exercise in building trust, fear, and obedience. Who did early moderns trust to teach the codes?

The Spanish did not invent Manila's grid of straight streets and sharp corners. While they had encountered it on a massive scale in Tenochtitlan, they borrowed the theory and practice from the Romans. Or reimagined it. Roman civil engineering in bridges, streets, and buildings was only the start. When early modern judiciaries undertook the legal engineering of patriarchy or enslavement, they drew on Roman laws. When teachers and social reformers undertook the moral governance of children, orphans, and the poor, they drew on Roman pedagogical treatises. The enclosures lining roads were only partly modeled on convents and monasteries; most were laboratories for the reengineering of human beings, tightly enclosed to more easily remove flaws of gender, race, disability, and so on. Roman cartography gave the Spanish some of the tools to reach Manila, and Roman urbanism set its squares and right angles. Florence, like so many other south European cities, had remnants of the same ancient grid fixed in its historical core but the corners were rounded and bent by centuries of daily life. Yet the grid was sharply defined in the series of new towns that Florentines built to control frontier territories in the 1300s and again with the new port of Livorno from the 1570s (Friedman 1988; Tazzara 2017).

Manila's sharper edges embody Rome's spatial rebirth, modeled on a grand scale in Spain's new imperial capital of Madrid and duplicated for centuries thereafter almost anywhere that Europeans went to settle and colonize. Nature might impose its own necessities – Amsterdam emerged long after the Romans had departed the marshy lowlands, and water shaped its patterns. The first English settlers to the Boston Bay area in 1629 laid out Charlestown on a flat shore with a Governor's great house anchoring a central square from which streets radiated out to accommodate settlement. After a rough summer the settlers moved across the river to establish Boston on the Shawmut peninsula, where inlets and hills made a grid impossible. Neither Amsterdam nor Boston initially had a natural setting for the Roman ideal of regimented and rectilinear spatial order, but both would embrace it fully in later suburban expansions. Boston even built a Roman triumphal arch to welcome George Washington in 1789 and staged a civic entry worthy of a Roman emperor (Peterson 2019). The Spanish were the most dogmatic in laying out colonial towns as a grid, deliberately reimagining Roman imperialism by sucking up multiple widely dispersed settlements into compact urban towns called "reductions" (*reducciónes* or *poblaciónes*) that looked like a legion's camp and were easier to defend and administer. When forcibly relocating Indigenous peoples in the Americas and Philippines into these new towns, the Spanish knew that a two-dimensional grid was not enough to shape the imagination. They erected stone churches and institutional buildings around main squares and extended stone walls around the whole, but also set the acoustic range of the church bell as the civic boundary. A grid might impose order, but it was spaces, volumes, and sound that moved the senses and shaped the imagination (Friedman 1988; Trachtenberg 1997).

Imitation was the sincerest form of flattery, and the Dutch copied both the Romans and Spanish as they moved into Asia. When the Dutch East India Company destroyed Jayakarta on Java and rebuilt it as their chief South Asian entrepôt in 1619–21, they surveyed the site as a grid and gave their new town the name that the Romans had given to the Netherlands: Batavia. From 1620 to 1650 they constructed a rigid grid of streets and squares offset by a fortress and surrounded by communities of Javanese and migrant Chinese and Japanese merchants who were forbidden to live within the walled compound. Unlike Manila's *Intramuros*, which Spanish authorities were coming to see as a remote and costly mistake, Batavia's walled *Kota* was a virtual extension of Amsterdam. And really an imitation of it as well. The East India Company (VOC) invested heavily to build Batavia to Dutch models with squares, churches, and tree-lined canals and streets. Agents and regents of the monopoly VOC kept close eyes on the trade that channeled unprecedented wealth back to the Netherlands and financed monumental structures in both cities (Taylor 1983; Kehoe 2023). Meanwhile, Manila declined both relatively and absolutely from the 1640s, and by the end of the eighteenth century counted only 1,500 Spanish and *mestizo* and perhaps 8,000 Tagalog and Chinese (Reyes 2017).

2.4 Sights of Power

The spire on a square had long been one of the major visualizations of the power of God, and towns and cities could spend centuries in building both. Religious reformers might speed the process and sometimes changed the theology but never forsook the impulse to give God the ultimate architectural glory with large spaces, ample light, and a directional spire. The humanist pope Pius II's project to rebuild his birthplace gave Europe its fastest cathedral construction (1459–62), a light-filled evocation of the Holy Spirit behind a pedimented Roman arch and facing a civic hall and two palaces across the square of the very tiny town of Pienza.

Regensburg's civic elite marked the death of Holy Roman Emperor Maximillian I in 1519 by expelling the Jews, razing the local ghetto and synagogue, and building the "New Parish" church on the ruins. From 1541 it became the symbolic and sonic center of the city's further Reformation. This hub of preaching and singing not only erased the Jews but also stalled work on a nearby cathedral long under construction and fated to wait for a nineteenth-century Catholic restoration before completion of *its* towers. The politics of religious reform might change theologies and alter designs, but they seldom abandoned the drive to give divine authority its appropriate spatial expression on city streets and squares. Regensburg's burghers were following the example of nearby Nuremburg, which had also demolished a synagogue and further erased its memory by building the Church of our Lady (*Frauenkirche*), a small relic-packed resonant hub throbbing with spiritual energy. Purgation was the first step of religious reform, as much spatially as theologically. While it would take a few decades for those overseeing Europe's various Protestant confessions to begin designing their own worship spaces, they wasted no time in purging Catholicism from the spaces they had inherited. Iconoclastic riots destroyed windows, altarpieces, and statutes. Whitewash erased the lessons formerly conveyed by frescoed images of saints and miracles. These mute visual cues disappeared from Protestant spaces so that preaching and song, long resonant in these spaces, could move to the foreground and give the message ever greater catechetical precision (Vanhaelen 2012). Catholic spaces also changed, but in ways that accentuated the senses: stuccoed figures stretched out from walls and ceilings, gilding teased in the half-light of candles, swirling ceiling trompe l'oeil frescoes blew away roofs to reveal the passage to heaven. But spatial specialization was also transforming these sometimes cavernous churches crammed with nooks and crannies where people had gathered for centuries to conduct business, sign contracts, or conduct liaisons both sacred and profane. While Protestant reformers were purging spaces of shrines and images altogether, Catholic reformers joined them in purging churches of secular activities and effectively professionalizing them as the workspaces of the clergy. These spaces had work to do in ushering souls to heaven. Clergy in Florence removed the rood screens that bisected the nave so that the whole interior space could be under surveillance and the activities within it could be monitored. English protestants erected fences around their altars to control the dogs whose barking, pissing, and interest in communion bread disturbed holy worship (Smith 2002; Craig 2005; Allen 2022).

Churches, convents, and monasteries had been among the most monumental spaces in medieval cities, giving sight of heaven both inside and out. Religious spaces gave visual form to a power that was abstract or metaphorical, the echo, image, or evocation of something transcendent. While castles, fortresses, and towers were hulking signs of an immediate physical power that could imprison, maim, or kill, churches conveyed a promise of transcendence – or eternal judgment – and used towers, windows, massive doors, and artwork to express these abstractions (Champion 2017). Guilds and governments borrowed these forms, giving some medieval institutional buildings a vaguely religious look. Architects also seized on Roman models, stretching long colonnades along the face of some institutions, setting arches at the entrances of others, and extending series of regularly spaced windows in heavy frames and pediments to bring light to public business in others. Even as antique ruins were being lost to looting in Rome and elsewhere, the new buildings of governments, institutions, and even companies were recreating new Romes across Europe and overseas.

Rome's visual imprint might be a monumental building, or sometimes only an elaborate facade. Yet these were necessary set pieces in the early modern theatre of power. The distinctive arcade of Florence's Innocenti orphanage, one of the key architectural designs of the early Renaissance, defined one side of a city square and inspired imitations on two other sides over the coming century and a half in an informal collaboration that created an unusually unified urban space. Monarchies were better able to plan and execute these schemes expeditiously than a merchant republic like Florence. Philip II demonstrated this truth with Madrid's Plaza Mayor from 1590 (completed 1614) and Henry IV did the same with the unified brick and stone facades ringing Paris' residential Place Royale from 1605. Their very scale and extravagant use of space spoke of the ambitions of both monarchs to turn their cities into royal capitals.

Occupying space was occupying power. The ability to *waste* space signaled even greater power in the cramped fabric of older cities. When Duke Cosimo de'Medici wanted to signal the end of the Florentine republic, he commissioned a new complex to house Florence's state magistracies in 1560, expropriating and demolishing a large block of houses belonging to some political enemies. Here he constructed new offices (*Uffizi*) in two connected wings flanking a broad open avenue/courtyard that extended the existing main civic square down to a classical arch overlooking the Arno river (1560–81). Duke Cosimo's own palace, connected to the new offices by a kilometer-long private corridor that elevated him above the public street, fronted an enormous public square on the main north/south road noted earlier. It opened to one of the first large formal Italian gardens behind. Kings, princes, and dukes across Europe followed suit with formal gardens featuring broad avenues, statues, fountains, and landscaped "rooms." Few topped their gardens with a fortress like the Medici's *Belvedere*, visible to all in the city below since its "good view" was engineered to give soldiers a clear line of fire over all the city (Trachtenberg 1997). Even republicans got into the business of wasting space to demonstrate power. Amsterdam's burghers marked the end of war with

Spain in 1648 by commissioning an enormous city hall: classically inspired, built of stone on a palatial scale, replete with globes and maps that visualized their empire, and planted in a vast public square in the heart of the city (Abrahamse 2019). Control of Asian wealth had made this monument possible, so in 1710 they built a smaller state house modeled on it in Batavia. The world was theirs.

   Boston came later to the game. What it lacked in the absence of powerful central authorities running Paris, Florence, or Amsterdam, it made up for in a widely held cultural consensus that believed classical architecture to be the canonical form for public buildings. Boston's King's Chapel (1689) was not officially a government building, but as the first Anglican Church built after the Puritans lost their monopoly on power it may as well have been; its classical portico signaled the new regime. Boston's State House (1713) held an exchange and market on the ground floor and the Governor's Council Chamber, the elected Assembly (General Court), and Supreme Judicial Court above. Christ Church rose a decade later, the oldest remaining of a series of Georgian or neoclassical churches by different denominations. In 1740–2 the slave merchant Peter Faneuil built a classically inspired market hall by the Town Dock. Boston had been the first colony to legalize slavery a century earlier in 1641 and its wharves and docks were the center of the New England trade in both African and Native American enslaved peoples (Peterson 2019). The enslaved arrived in this space and transited through it as though they were commodities rather than human beings. Yet Bostonians imagined that the serene and solid classical forms legitimated their power and commerce and advertised that, as with Batavia and Manila, here was a European civilization in the making. The key goal was to reproduce the spaces of the colonial metropole on a distant shore so that the economic, political, and cultural links would never be lost from sight, even if for some of those passing through, these spaces were links in a very different set of chains.

3 The Force of Sound

How far does the sound of a bell travel? The bigger the bell, the deeper the sound, and the further its reach. In modern cities the peal of a bell competes with a packed register of background noises: cars and buses moving by, planes overhead, construction machinery, sirens, and even distant factories, all of them steadily reducing the range of our bell's sound. We're so accustomed to these noises that we may not even consciously hear them unless we stop to listen. Even so, the soundwaves of a single distant bell will be flattened and lost in a fog of ambient noise.

Preindustrial cities were generally quieter places using forms of communication that we simply can't hear anymore. Bells most of all, which explains the cupolas atop the city halls of Boston, Amsterdam, and Batavia, the competing towers of church and state in Florence, and the squat but resonant bell tower of Manila's cathedral. But at the opposite end of the sonic spectrum, voices also had range. Town criers were a real thing. Preachers filled public squares with the range of their own voices extended by distant listeners who heard and passed on the message. Sentences of execution announced from gallows reached the edges of squares where audiences gathered to watch the theatre of punishment. On the opposite side, plaques attached to the outer walls of convents threatened fines on those Florentines whose soccer playing, singing, or lovemaking might disturb the meditative silence imposed on the women held inside. Mapping the soundscapes of early modern cities is about more than separating noise from sound or tracing the sonic cartography of bells and voices. It's about recreating those acoustic communities that gathered and defined themselves by instruments and voices and listening to the life they shared. It's also about discerning acoustic horizons, measuring how sound captured, plotted, and purged public spaces, and imagining how music and language animated private relations.

3.1 Sonic Messaging

In 1498, after Florentines had burned the religious reformer Girolamo Savonarola and swept his ashes into the Arno, they climbed the bell tower of his Dominican house of San Marco and dislodged its great bell, the *Piagnona*. They pulled the bell through the city on an ox cart, whipping it steadily for having violated civic peace when it summoned Savonarola's disciples to events like bonfires of the vanities. Those working the whips counted on their bells to provide order. Naming them was not just a sign of civic pride or affection, but a recognition that bells marked the grid of time. They had to be dependable and predictable, and so were held accountable (Zolli and Brown 2019). A century and a half earlier, the start of the workers' rebellion known as the *Ciompi* Revolt had been signaled through these same streets when the sequence of bells sounding a civic alarm had been rung out of order. The correct sequence marking daily life was so ingrained and recognizable that something as simple as ringing bells out of order was enough to send workers into the streets in recognition that civic order was breaking down. The biggest bell in Florence's civic palace, the *Leone* or *Grosso*, sounded deepest and furthest. For over two centuries it was the first civic bell to open the day and the last to close it. More importantly, it also rang at times when the republic was threatened, summoning citizens to rush to the main civic square for a *parlamento* or to defend the spaces, structures, and constitution of the Florentine republic. Two years after his appointment by the Holy Roman Emperor, whose siege had finally broken that republic, the first Duke of Florence, Alessandro de'Medici, had the *Leone* removed and ceremonially broken to pieces in front of him in the square, silencing what one contemporary called its "sweet sound of liberty" (Atkinson 2016, 65–7).

Can a bell be accountable, or hold to account? Because they sounded rarely but regularly, bells were the most common and dependable governors marking individual and communal obligations. Medieval bells had marked the eight hours of prayer from before dawn to sundown when clergy were to pray. A small bell rang as the priest consecrated the host in communion. Disputes over the rights of muezzins to issue the call to prayer were among the sonic weapons used by religious polemicists in fifteenth-century Iberian intercommunal politics (Tolan 2005). These sonic measures of spiritual accountability conversed with bells central to civic timekeeping, making it imperative that they be heard across town (Champion 2017). A complex sequence of larger and smaller bells sounded the opening and closing of markets, courts, and civic offices in most towns, as this was the only reliable way to mark time when few people owned or were in sight of clocks. When Amsterdam extended its boundaries with new canals and streets it constructed new churches as a public good. Time and space governed church planting and naming after the euphemistically named "Alteration" of 1578 when the Catholic city council was deposed. Over the coming decades the Protestant civic government built three new churches to supplement the cavernous Old Church (1306) near the sea to the northeast and New Church (1409) on the central Dam Square. Their prosaic names reflected the mix of sacred and secular function: the South Church (1603–11), the North Church (1620–3), and, grandest of all, the West Church (1620–31). These marked urban space as clearly as numbers on a clock face. While their prominent steeples featured clocks, it was their bells that counted most, summoning believers for Sunday worship and keeping time day in and out for those living and working in the newer neighborhoods by ringing every quarter hour. The Reformed State Church marked public time as a public responsibility. While Anabaptists and even Catholics could have places of worship, these were to be hidden out of sight in courtyards or attics and above all out of hearing without bells. They had no public function and so made no public sound.

But the sound of bells rang out for more than just religious obligations or civic time keeping. In rural Piedmont in northern Italy, village feasts were open to whoever might hear the bells announcing them. When Spanish colonizers forced Indigenous peoples into the planned villages or *reducciónes*, they established the acoustic range of the parish bell as the boundary of the civil community. Some historians have thought that the same acoustic sensibility set the bounds of rural parishes (Torre 1995, 2019).

For all their force, most bells were heavy and fixed, with a limited expressive range. Brass was the necessary mobile counterpart to bells when it came to public announcements. Publicly commissioned town criers moved around the city giving news, announcements, warnings, and appeals, sometimes accompanied by drummers and trumpeters who commanded the pause that allowed them to be heard (see Figure 5). Puritan Governor William Bradford brought a drummer and trumpeter when meeting King Massasoit to discuss peace in 1620. By mid-century, towns in the new Massachusetts Bay colony were fined if they failed to have a trumpet or drum to call citizens to meetings, announce laws, or share news (Hoover 1985). In sixteenth-century Bologna, the second largest public expense was for musicians, exceeded only by the cost of maintaining soldiers, and likely more useful for keeping public order. Amsterdam's night watch groups carried small brass rattles to raise help when encountering lawbreakers on the darkened streets.

Figure 5 Town Crier. Cornelis Ploos van Amstel, 1776 (National Gallery of Art, Washington)

Town criers' instrument was the voice, and their competition too. Peddlers cried their wares in market squares, street stalls, mobile carts, or as they walked through towns. The larger a town, the greater the number of those circulating through its streets calling out their pamphlets and broadsheets, the barrels of wine they carried on their backs, the vegetables or fish they pushed on carts. They seized attention with rhymes, taunts, and teasing and counted on their voices to draw in customers. Marketing was verbal, a performance art, whether from stalls or on the streets. Vendors with shops might have a visual sign or symbol above their door, but more sellers used sonic means to announce their goods and prices, much as modern ones use radio or social media.

Marketers' voices continued down every street with conversations, songs, and performances that reveled in rhymes and dialects; not all messaging had a public or commercial purpose. London theatres featured city comedies where a playwright like Thomas Dekker imitated the Dutch or Portuguese-accented voices heard on the streets to roaring approval as immigrant characters were bested in games of love or commerce by native-speaking English (Rubright 2014). Amsterdam entertainments included lotteries where ticket buyers had to write a doggerel rhyming poem to accompany their entry; when tickets were drawn, the poems were read out loud to the laughs and groans of the audience. It could take days of round the clock recitation – the rules of this game were that every ticket had to be drawn, and every poem read (Puttevils 2017). Voices commanded attention and patience: buy a broadsheet or pamphlet from a walking peddler, and you might take it to a tavern or coffeehouse to read it aloud to others there, triggering laughs, debates, jeers, or applause (Smith 1999). Reading was a silent practice for only a few, and a public performance for many, vastly extending the reach of the pamphlets, news briefs, and prophecies that were pouring out of presses in cities everywhere. In migrant neighborhoods these voices read out home languages and mother tongues: about a quarter of those living in fast-growing eighteenth-century Berlin were Huguenot religious refugees speaking French, and public readings reinforced the pronunciations and cadences they gave their children in weekly Sunday School sessions. Migrant voices and different languages sent a message of community and belonging, particularly to those with more limited public roles like children and women. These again bent the binaries of insider and outsider that some public authorities aimed to proclaim. Or to enforce. Many enclosures for children that aimed to engineer new citizens began with language: elite boarding schools in Boston and Amsterdam formed ruling classes by means of vernacular accents and professional languages like Latin. Colonial mission schools in Manila and Quebec erased Indigenous identities and networks by punishing the use of mother tongues, a practice that extended well into the twentieth century (Graham 2019).

3.2 Sonic Purging

When Naples was hit with plague in 1656, authorities took an expensive but necessary step for public sanitation: they loaded cannons with empty charges of gunpowder and blew them over the city. Medical experts had assured them that the cannon blasts would clear away the heavy layer of disease-ridden malaria – literally bad air – that lay over Naples like a suffocating blanket and bring in fresh air to revive the population. Or so the theory went.

It was the noise from the cannon's mouth that cleared the air, not just the burst of flame and blast of compressed air. It was commonly believed that lower rates of plague in the coppersmith's quarter of Dijon owed less to hygiene than to the steady banging of hammers on metal and the fire that both kept rats away (Galanaud and Galanaud 2020). Doctors in Naples went further, trying to determine how sound entered the body as a physical force and affected the bodily constitution. They were tracing the *physical* force and biological impact of sound long before theories of sound waves developed. Bodies amazed and perplexed them, and the standard Galenic theory of the humors – the balance of four fluids (blood, phlegm, yellow and black bile) in our bodies that fluctuated with age, gender, disposition, diet, and host of other factors and that governed physical and emotional health – provided an opening for sound as medicine, remedy, and perhaps even infection (Rombough 2024).

Sound in the form of music had long been thought to move the body by means of the emotions – humoral balancing was a delicate art combining emotions and rest with biology and diet. Classical authors found music almost subversive in its effects on emotions, and the Biblical shepherd David had soothed the troubled spirit of King Saul with his lyre and psalms. David's sonic purgation of the king was not enough to change Saul's heart in the end, perhaps because the king couldn't hear and share the larger narrative of repentance and obedience that David's psalms voiced. In the early years of reformation, Protestants in some cities like Amsterdam and Boston allowed only those sung psalms as the musical expression of worship, silencing even instruments. They were wary of the power of song and verse to move emotions. Yet David's psalms were employed in spiritual purgations critical to dramatic displays of public justice like public executions. Sensory rituals juxtaposing sound and silence bridged the emotional and physical sides of punishment for both the condemned and the audiences witnessing their death (Craig 2005).

Boston, Amsterdam, and Florence all raised gallows outside the city walls because the execution of a murderer, a counterfeiter, or heretic was a purgation removing the condemned from *urbs* and *civitas*. Executions had elaborate sensory rituals differing from city to city and from one condemned to another.

Some cities closed shops and offices on these days and rang the city bells to bring out witnesses for the expulsion and execution. Audiences were not mute spectators in the highly public theatre of punishment. Jeers and catcalls greeted some of the condemned and wails of sorrow and mercy greeted others. Purgation of the condemned included a public reading of the charges and the condemned's own gallows confession or cries along the route (Terpstra 2008). Amsterdam conducted executions from a wooden platform extending from a window at the front of its monumental City Hall, where prisons, torture rooms, and courts were all located. A bell summoned citizens to witness public justice, and after the condemned had prayed together with the magistrates who were putting him to death, he stepped out the window to meet the executioner. Only after death were some bodies moved, without ceremony, to rot on the public gallows outside the city; about half of those executed made it here (Gobin 2021). Differing sounds of execution in Boston demonstrated another distinction made by colonial societies. Puritan authorities executed European Christians like the four Quaker "Boston Martyrs" by hanging (1659–61). In the wake of the 1676 war with the Wampanoag sachem Metacom (also known as King Phillip), they shot fifty Native American captives, some of them Christians, possibly at the gallows just outside the city gate. After a hanging, Bostonians simply dumped the corpses on the ground for either some charitable soul to bury them or animals to consume; it's not clear what happened to the executed Wampanoag.

These were not the only sounds of public justice. Music was used selectively and effectively. Inquisitorial executions like the grand autos-da-fé held in Madrid's Plaza Major in 1680 shut out the cacophonous crowds and restricted access to sober elites and clergy arranged in ranks on benches lining the square (see Figure 6). Their control of their own emotions and obedience to Catholic decorum were expressed in choral performances, in the public recantations of some condemned, and in the slow burning of others who refused to bend. This inquisitorial practice highlights a second level of purgation that was to happen *inside* the condemned. Florentines, like many Italians, brought music into this process as robed and hooded confraternity brothers worked with a range of sensory tools to save the condemned's soul, beginning in the prison cell the night before execution. They brought images of martyred saints directly before his eyes, whispered stories of miraculous interventions into his ears, and tutored him with psalm litanies of confession and remorse. One of the most memorable and popular songs punctuated a long series of confessions with the cry "Misericordia" (mercy), which they chanted down the long route to execution outside the city walls. Capturing his senses to shut out the crowd and securing his verbal confession in a psalm, poem, or gallows confession brought purgation

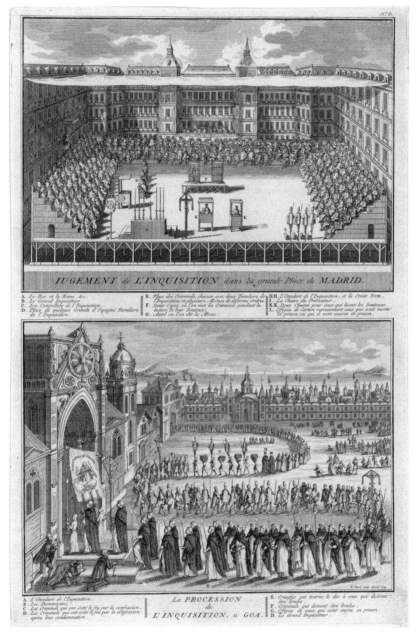

Figure 6 Auto-da-fé in Madrid and Goa. Bernard Picart, 1723 (Rijksmuseum)

full circle, for his admission of guilt and acceptance of punishment would set him on the road to heaven. Adding the taste of the eucharistic host, the light of candles, and the smell of incense and sweat resulted in a complete somaesthetic experience, with the criminal's body and senses becoming critical to the rituals (Terry 2010; Terpstra 2015a). Or so the theory went.

The doctors might return after these execution rituals and take the body to study it more closely; criminals were a common source of corpses for anatomy lessons. Bologna's university anatomy theatre had a direct and convenient connection to the confraternity that comforted condemned prisoners. Its medical students paid for additional masses to be sung for the souls of those condemned who consented to this use of their corpses. Its curious elites bought tickets to witness the anatomical exercises, perhaps wondering like the doctors whether the force of the sounds around the execution had left physical marks inside the body laid out before them (Terpstra 2008).

3.3 Sounds of Faith

Executions were among the most extreme events that merged public performance and individual pain through sensory evocations of Christ's death. Baying crowds fell silent when the executioner stepped forward to do his work, but the spiritual referents gave additional meaning and emotional power to the noisy work of axe, noose, or gun. When some Protestant religious reformers curbed music in worship, it was because they were conscious of how quickly the emotions of the moment could crowd out a message. Catholics had long thought that intensifying the message with emotion was precisely the point, and nothing was more sensory and emotional than the death of Christ. Through Holy Week, the seven days leading up to the commemoration of Christ's Good Friday crucifixion and Easter resurrection, Catholic towns like Florence and Manila buzzed with preparations. Holy Week was the most resonant point of the liturgical year, far outstripping Christmas. Squares and churches filled with those who'd come to listen to star preachers brought in for the occasion. These played the crowd like a violin, evoking Christ's anger at his enemies, his sorrow at the betrayal of his disciples, his silence under torture, and his cries at death (Mesquida 2018). The lay brothers of Rome's Gonfalone confraternity staged Passion plays in the ruins of the Coliseum, while merchants and artisans of English and Flemish altar guilds presented mystery plays on carts dragged on to streets as movable stages (Wisch and Newbiggin 2013). The full register of shouts and calls for mediation or action sent Christians into the streets, some shaking donation boxes to raise funds for the poor, others calling for repentance as they whipped themselves in imitation of Christ and recreated his long and painful progress to execution outside Jerusalem. Others bayed for vengeance against those the preachers claimed had betrayed or mocked Christ with their very lives: prostitutes, gay men, Jews. Piety roared as some sought local blood for Jesus' blood. They raced down red light districts, broke into homes, vandalized synagogues, rioted and beat up any targets who hadn't locked down or fled town days before. When it came to marking the death of the Lord, lay religion was not restrained and orderly but riotous, loud, and bloody, not shy of recreating the violence of Christ's flagellation.

Public piety was mobile, rhythmic, and sensory. The steadily intensifying performative spirituality of Holy Week followed forty days of quiet fasting, prayer, and reflection on sin known as Lent, which itself had been launched with the riotous days of Carnival in February. Forty days after Easter came Ascension Day, marking Christ's return to heaven. Twenty days later the great processions of Corpus Domini celebrated Christ's regular return in the miracle of transubstantiation, as he became really present to believers when the priest consecrated the host in the mass. The most intense public events of the Catholic year clustered into the first six months, with physical and sensory rituals recreating the intensely emotional progress of Christ's life and death through local streets, squares, and shrines. Festivals in the rest of the year tended to be more celebrative and inclusive expressions of acoustic community: saints' days sent believers out together to shrines, All Souls brought them into cemeteries, and the feasts of their patrons brought them around the city in processions moving to the rhythm of song. Lay religion was broadly participatory. Confraternal processions by free and enslaved Black Africans in Brazil were among the only public events permitted them by Portuguese authorities, precisely to demonstrate the universality of the Catholic Church (Muir 2005; Fromont 2019; Monroe 2023). Manila had fourteen patron saints, and their festivals drew in both Chinese and Japanese merchants and Tagalog converts to follow bands and blow off fireworks. Processions were celebratory and collective occasions marking a wide range of Manila's communal life. Members of all communities processed to celebrate every time a new galleon was launched or when one sailed or returned from the long voyage to Acapulco (Reyes 2017; Mesquida 2018).

The festive life of cities always brought together rituals of cohesion and rituals of separation in crazy juxtaposition. Catholic religious reformers had seized on the participatory and sensory side of processions, which they saw as no less effective than cannons at purifying the civic air and space. This made the sound of singing, whips, and instruments controversial; Savonarola's bell had paid the price for calling people to action. The pyres he erected for his bonfires of vanities included musical scores and instruments among stacks of paintings, books, and playing cards. His followers were so well known for their loud wailing that they earned the sniggering tag of "weepers" (*piagnoni*), which was no compliment in decorous Florence. Catholic priests in France used eucharistic processions to track down Huguenots, who risked popular assault if they failed to bow as the Host passed by. Anabaptist reformers in Amsterdam had attempted their own purgation, stripping naked and preaching and singing through the city in January 1526 to demonstrate a new life with nothing to hide. All ended up on the gallows. Amsterdam's Protestant "Alteration" of 1578 put an end to Catholic punishments and processions alike, but reformers continued to emphasize the public and sonic side of their message and evoke biblical models for it.

The New Testament book of Acts recorded the sound of a rushing wind at Pentecost, when Peter preached to crowds in Jerusalem who each heard in their own language. This was the preacher's charter, regardless of confession. Mendicant friars had long filled public squares and built their enormous basilicas dedicated to their patrons like St Francis or St Dominic to be theatres for preaching. Public bible reading and long sermons explicating biblical texts continued as the centerpiece of worship in Amsterdam, Boston, and other Protestant cities. It was the only licit entertainment; the same Protestant reformers who closed theatres were suspicious of instrumental music. Boston's puritans banned it from worship and heated debates kept organs out of Amsterdam's new and towering churches for decades after their construction (Lambert 1985). Singing David's psalms became the most common form of public participation in worship services where attendance was required and monitored, and absences were punished. While the Protestant psalms were known in some quarters as "Genevan jigs," many were methodical, metrical, and slow. This ensured that the biblical message of the text was not obscured by melodies, and that complex harmonies did not put human invention into competition with the Word of God. Not all reformers were quite so austere. Martin Luther understood the draw of singing to his message and put religious texts to popular tunes to help their spread. Thomas Tallis remained Catholic but composed in tune with the religious proclivities of the four monarchs for whom he wrote: complex polyphony under Henry VIII and later Mary I, anthems with simpler tunes and straightforward comprehensible biblical texts and melodies under Edward VI, and a skillful merging of polyphonic art and Book of Common Prayer teaching under Elizabeth I. For many churchgoers regardless of confession, music was a more immediate and compelling expression of faith than sermons, images, or tracts (Bertoglio 2017; Willis 2018).

All religious reformers understood that public music brought a powerful and persuasive force of sound to the gospel. Protestants tended to be wary of letting emotive tunes or texts disturb the simple purity of the gospel message. Catholic confraternities continued leading emotional public singing in processions and churches, but choirs played a larger role in voicing the complex harmonies and Latin texts of the mass. As the schism between confessions widened, their preferences became more important to building their respective acoustic communities and the image they fashioned of themselves. Congregational singing of biblical texts in the vernacular became the defining mark of Protestantism's orientation to lay-driven participatory worship. Choral melodies accentuated the performative theatre of witnessing the Catholic Mass. The distinctions in practice weren't always so pronounced. Catholic missions outside Europe found vernacular singing critical to winning conversion, while musicians whom Protestants favored like Bach and Handel composed cantatas and oratorios that professional singers performed for appreciative patrons and congregations. The oratorio was a new musical form that bridged confessions and jumped to the secular world as opera, which was a highly popular and public art form before being enclosed in elite theatres (Brown 2005; Bertoglio 2017; Filippi and Noone 2017).

Confraternities of Africans in Kongo and Latin America formed acoustic communities with drumming, wind and string instruments, and spiritual exercises in their own languages (Fromont 2019; Valerio 2022; Monroe 2023). Franciscans in rural Mexico were far more successful than their rival Dominicans in gaining converts since they fostered the brotherhoods as sites for local vernaculars (Dirksmeir 2020). Ironically, a similar distinction separated image from reality in southern France: while Protestant Huguenots purported to value lay and vernacular worship, they tended to use the standard French of the educated and professional classes, while Catholic missionaries preaching in local dialects proved more effective in reaching the common people.

3.4 Sonic Governance

When brothers and sisters in Black Brazilian confraternities drummed and danced at their gatherings and in procession, they were continuing pious practices rooted in West African Catholicism that made their brotherhoods powerful sites of identity (Dempsey 2018; Monroe 2023; see Figure 7). English planters on the Barbados weren't thrilled with the sound of drumming coming from encampments of the Africans they'd enslaved. It terrorized them, particularly at night, when they feared it might be the sound of revolt. Their Protestant faith shut down the confraternities, and their colonizers' fears shut down the drumming, but the sounds of the night weren't so easily policed.

In smaller towns and rural villages, it was a commonplace that youths ruled the night, and under cover of darkness they governed with sound. Carousing in

Figure 7 Afonso I of Kongo giving an audience. Anon (Wikimedia Commons)

taverns or on streets where sex workers gathered was a given. Popular tunes gained new verses inspired by local scandals, wars, or politics, and sea shanties moved with sailors from port to port. It was entertainment that needed no light or literacy, or even a singing voice. Florence's Office of Decency put a priority on controlling the singing and shouting around brothels and, apart from assault, carousing (*baccano*) was the biggest cause of the fines it levied on men (Terpstra 2015c). Boston officials in 1664 came down heavily on groups of young men singing rude songs (Hoover 1985, 766).

Youths' sounds could be forceful and pointed. Rough music, *charivari*, and *mattinata* were just some of the terms every language had to describe the mix of yelling, yodeling, pot banging, and singing youths used, usually at night, to acoustically punish or taunt those who had set themselves outside social expectations. The old widower who married a young girl, the priest's servant who became his concubine, the groom who couldn't conceive, the merchant who hoarded grain in a famine, the baker who trimmed the size of his loaves, the master who reneged on paying his journeymen, the woman or man who beat their spouse, the Protestant in a Catholic town or vice versa. There was no shortage of those whose actions aggravated their neighbors but whose position or power made it dangerous – or pointless – to bring them to law. Many hadn't even broken any written laws. Yet they lived or acted outside of social expectations. The whispered complaints, gossip, and grievances of adults summoned youths to conduct their policing under cover of night with penalties ranging from simple shaming to physical violence and vandalism. Pots and pans banged outside the windows of a May–December wedding for nights on end until a bag of coins tossed into the street paid the fine; a shop's shutters were broken repeatedly till the merchant saw the light of fair pricing; a young groom was pulled from bed and paraded around town in mocking costume till he fulfilled expectations. Having adolescent boys police morality could get dark, and not just at night. In vendetta-riven Friuli, the dead and murdered might be pulled from their graves and dragged around town while drums beat and baying dogs and pigs feasted on the flesh. The brothels of Dijon were filled with young women who had been "disciplined" with sexual assaults by gangs of youths. When feeling confident, these might act during the daytime, as when Protestant youths in a Swiss village burst into a Catholic service, loudly disrupting the service and roughing up the priest (Rossiaud 1988; Cashmere 1991; Muir 1998, 2005). And at certain times of year, like Carnival or Maytime, gangs of singing and dancing youths led the parades and festivities celebrating fertility or harvest. Darkness and youth were critical protections; those under fourteen typically suffered only a fraction of the adult penalty. In many cases adults willingly looked the other way while their sons and nephews administered rough justice. Verbal cues triggered the violence, which was delivered with the full sonic register. Rough justice was a sensory tool operating beyond the reach of printed law codes and using social sounds to enforce social expectations. Sounds reminded people where and who they were, and whether they belonged. When Florentines forced Jews into a ghetto, they designated the city block holding its still-functioning civic brothel, thereby ensuring that Jewish Sabbath silence would be broken constantly by the Saturday din of young men carousing loudly on their only day off.

But back to David's lyre. Not all music was either rough or pious (see Figure 8). When Antonio Vivaldi composed for and trained the orphaned and abandoned girls at Venice's Pietà conservatory, their public performances drew large crowds that helped keep the orphanage afloat. Colleagues at similar shelters for boys in Bologna trained their wards as public mourners hired out for funeral processions (Baldauf-Berdes 1996). Handel composed his oratorio "Messiah" in part to fund orphanages in Dublin and London. Music was big business. From the sixteenth century, Florence's economy drew more income from instrument makers, choral composers, music teachers and copyists than it ever did from painters and sculptors. Because music was for those who had everything, it became a means of mobility for those who had nothing. Orphan boys took their instrumental skills into military regiments and their singing skills into local choirs and theatres. Some became highly paid *castrati*; those

Figure 8 The concert. Gerrit van Honthorst, 1623 (National Gallery of Art, Washington)

who weren't orphans almost always came from poor families (Finucci 2003). Vivaldi's female musicians might move into marriages or the convent, but they had fewer opportunities outside the conservatory to exercise their music skills or earn a living from them (Baldauf-Berdes 1996).

A more common form of mobility was dancing. Fiddles were a portable and prized accompaniment to dancing at fairs, parties, and taverns. A popular genre of Dutch art depicted the singing, dancing, and carousing in taverns and outdoor feasts that persisted despite, or perhaps because of, the strictures of Reformed preachers. Those strictures may be a stereotype. Colonial Boston inventories record a host of fiddles, carried over with dance traditions from England. Dancing passed the Puritan test by being mentioned in the book of Exodus – at least some dancing. John Cotton, grandfather of Cotton Mather, denounced "lascivious dancing to wanton ditties and in amorous gestures and wanton dalliances, especially after great feasts" but gave thumbs up to religious dance (Howard 1985, 731–2). Puritans put many boundaries around recreation, and in Boston even briefly banned bowling. Yet they came from a strong musical culture that animated the homes and streets of Boston (Lambert 1985, 411; Bagley, 2021).

4 The Sites of Smell

When Amsterdam's canals froze over in the winter it was a bit of a relief. Not the cold itself, which gripped Europe throughout the seventeenth century, the worst period of the Little Ice Age. Many North Europeans came to know what it was like to live in Canada without actually moving there. Despite freezing in their homes and seeking some relief through stoves, Amsterdammers were relieved when sheets of ice sealed in the smell of their canals. Canals reeked of shit. While tides and the Amstel River did their best to flush them out, the sheer number of people crowding into the booming city and the inevitability of still backwaters here and there made it inevitable that human waste would overpower nature's ability to carry it away. To live in Amsterdam was to smell shit.

The sites that smell produced were not readily avoidable. Seasonal shifts accelerated or slowed decomposition of human and animal waste. They affected social policy and individual action when bad air was fingered as the cause of diseases ranging from plague to syphilis that often expanded in summer and declined in winter. Alternate strong smells were considered medically effective, as when Florentine health authorities used vinegar to dispel unhealthy miasmas and sanitize quarantined spaces or Amsterdam smokers used tobacco to dry up moist humors. Smell was also a sensory index of holiness and evil in religious life – from incense in worship and the odor of sanctity in saint-making, on one hand, to the revulsion around sulfur and stench as the olfactory calling card of the devil, on the other. Colonialism gave an expanded olfactory range and meaning to daily experience like the profits involved in the smells of camphor and benzoin in Manila, of nutmeg, mace, and coffee in Amsterdam, or of fish in Boston. Smell was an index of difference and became more prominent as a marker of social and racial distinction, through both the smells of food and cultural practices and body odor.

4.1 Smells of Decay

We began with the toilet and should perhaps get it out of the way first. Amsterdam was not the only city wrapped and trapped in the smell of human and animal waste. It was a travelers' commonplace that you would smell a town before you ever saw it. Cities on rivers and harbors turned to flowing water to wash away as much as possible. Amsterdam's locational advantage where a river met a tidal bay may have led it to trust too much in the flushing powers of that flowing water and so it ran sewers directly from houses into the canals (Abrahamse 2019). Manila's Chinese Sangleyes Parian and Japanese Dilau neighborhoods were even more congested and sent the waste flushed into the Pasig river directly downstream to wash and waft around the walls of the Spanish *Intramuros*. Boston relied on privies, which had to be cleaned out regularly, and ensured that the bodily smells were never far from home. A 1701 regulation required these be at least twelve feet from the road and at least six feet underground to preserve the health of those passing by (Bagley 2021). Bostonians might dig their privy in a back yard but a Londoner like Samuel Pepys writes long and passionately about his fights with a next door neighbor over spillover from the adjoining pits underneath their homes. Cleaning privies was wretched and smelly work undertaken by "gong farmers" and the euphemistic name "night-soil" gives an idea of the preferred time of day for this to happen. Older and smaller towns might not have the luxury of privies; an English village regulated how high residents might pile the dung they put in the streets outside their doors, while London authorities fined those who emptied their chamber pots out the window rather than thoughtfully bringing them down to street level to deposit directly in the gutter (Logue 2021).

One sensory reality remained: as temperatures rose, so did the smells. There were a host of medical, physiological, and biological reasons why plagues tended to increase in summer and decrease in winter, but most city dwellers followed their noses when deciding what to blame. Summer heat increased the olfactory intensity of the bad air, or *mal-aria*, that Neapolitan authorities had attempted to disperse with cannon fire. When it lingered and settled, accentuated by the smoke of household fires and the pungent leavings of butchers, fishmongers, and grocers, the stew of noxious particles emitted by human and animal waste became the blanketing miasma that city dwellers feared most of all. Among the many diverse theories circulating in early sixteenth century to explain the sudden appearance of syphilis in Naples in the 1490s, one fingered the bad air circulating around the city at the time. There, as in Amsterdam, Manila, and Boston, winds over the water would come eventually (Newson 2009). Florentine elites didn't spend summers at their rural villas for the landscape alone. Caught in the Arno Valley with hills around, Florentines inhaled a stagnant miasma that built steadily in the still summer heat. Like many landlocked and desperate people, they fought fire with fire. When plague hit, they locked and quarantined the homes of those who died and cleaned them with strong vinegar so that an antiseptic smell could replace the smell of putrefaction and death (Henderson 2019). Most landlocked cities did the same, and they did it most often when under a stifling summer miasma. Even port cities adopted quarantine as a matter of course. Large dormitory warehouses outside their ports – and in the case of Venice, two islands set apart in the lagoon in 1423 and 1468 – were the obligatory enclosures greeting merchants and sailors on any ship arriving from a place suspected of having plague. Plague doctors in some cities wore early modern airtight hazmat suits with long black robes, gloves, wide brimmed hats, and facemasks with glass eyepieces and long noses stuffed with mixtures of cleansing spices, herbs, and flowers like ambergris, cloves, mint, myrrh, lavender, or roses to purify the contaminated air they had to breathe (Stevens Crawshaw 2016; Glatter and Finkelman 2021).

Plague intensified an olfactory problem that cities faced day-to-day: what to do with the bodies of those who had died? Like dung, these were often remarkably close at hand. The cavernous churches in Florence that mendicant friars had built as auditoria for preaching were funded in large part by the bequests of those buried under their floors at financial rates that increased the closer one came to the main altar. The floors of Amsterdam's old and new city churches were a series of gravestones used as pavers with the wealthiest remembered by name, size, and carved artwork; the poor lay in mass graves accessed by a single practical stone. Amsterdam's Old Church alone had roughly 10,000 buried under 2,500 paver tombstones, and the courtyards of Manila's convents and beaterias held the bodies of the nuns who had died there. The courtyards of hospitals, orphanages, and foundling homes in all these cities held the bodies of those who had died inside. Officials and the wealthy might have a marker, but children and the poor were simply piled in anonymously, layer upon layer, or in the case of Florence's Innocenti foundling home, shoved under the monumental portico (Leader 2023).

Smaller and newer towns like Boston had graveyards outside their churches. The bigger step was to relocate graveyards outside the city walls, a move made unthinkable to many because this was where the cursed bodies of heretics and Jews had always been dumped (see Figure 9). But with space running out, churches becoming insufferably smelly, and corpses adding to summer mias- mas, cities contemplated turning to locating graveyards in distant parts of the city or outside the walls altogether. Paris, London, Florence, and Amsterdam would not take this move until the late eighteenth or early nineteenth century. We can't underestimate how emotionally and spiritually serious it was to cease burying the dead within the church, convent, or hospital that had sheltered them, promised to remember them in death, and stood ready to greet them at the resurrection that Christians anticipated at the end of time. Protestant theology broke the promise and hold of the dead as those who might help the living reach heaven through appropriate requiems and remembrances. Yet many of those who abandoned Catholicism continued to prefer resting places close to and preferably inside the church (Koslofsky 2000; Roberts 2000). Only the miasmic stench of death hanging over a city's churches and hospitals could lead author- ities to break their pact with dead in order to safeguard the lives of the living.

4.2 Smells of the Body

Some bodies didn't simply smell after death; in some cases they stank long before. While smell was the key index of health, many were content to smell

Figure 9 Jewish burial. Romeyn de Hooghe, c. 1695 (Rijksmuseum)

awful. Wampanoag, Iroquois, and Wendat in the Americas commonly complained of the stench put out by the French and English. Japanese and Chinese made the same complaints about the Spanish and Portuguese. It wasn't a case of long months at sea without laundry, but a combination of different diets and habits of hygiene. The meat-heavy diets of European male traders and soldiers contributed in part to the stronger smells they emitted. They barely noticed it in each other, but it immediately assaulted those outside of Europe eating diets of fish, fruits, and vegetables. Most of those whom Europeans encountered also valued cleanliness more than Europeans did and bathed more frequently. Native Americans, East Asians, and Ottomans all developed sophisticated cultures around bathing and invested significant resources securing hot water, communal spaces, and time. Indigenous North Americans built sweat lodges and bathed in rivers and streams. Unlike bearded and hairy European men, they preferred smooth and clear skin. Buddhist and Shinto culture both valued purification, and the Japanese used various forms of steam baths in communal bathhouses (*sento*) where men, women, and children bathed together; some also enjoyed heated tubs (*suefuro*) for individual cleaning. Social bathing cleared the spirit as it cleaned the body, and it spread so widely among all classes that it was one of the things that European travelers to China commented on with

Figure 10 Hamman. Anon, seventeenth century (Wellcome Collection)

perplexity and judgment. Large public bathhouses also spread in the Song (1270–1368) and Ming (1368–1644) dynasties, with barbering, massages, scrubbing, and personal grooming. The Ottoman *hammans* (see Figure 10) were among the most elaborate bathhouses where steam rooms, cold baths, massages, and conversation turned bathing into a social event (Ward 2019).

Europeans saw and experienced these bathhouses and wrote about them extensively in travel books. Closer to home the *hammans* in Granada, Girona, Valencia, and a host of other Iberian cities were in regular use until the wide-ranging expulsions of Muslims in 1609–14. The educated knew how much the ancient Romans and Greeks had valued bathing and could see when they poked over the ruins of ancient Roman towns that the largest structures with the most complicated engineering were the ancient baths. All religious traditions incorporated physical and spiritual purification into the rituals of approaching God. Muslims carried out the ritual purification of *wudu* before prayers, washing face, arms, head, and feet. Jews ritually purified themselves regularly either with two-handled *natla* cups or by immersion in *mikveh* baths connected to naturally flowing water. Christian religious rituals equated central sacraments like baptism with bathing, and the language of salvation was one of cleansing. This makes European Christian resistance to the global culture of bathing – and their resulting stench – all the harder to understand. Forms of bathhouse culture had long existed across Europe, although in the fifteenth century these became associated with brothels and indeed were often places where eating, drinking and sex were all on offer. Their linking of physical cleanliness with sexual activity pushed women and children from client to service roles and limited their use on gender lines. It also made it easier for authorities to close them as moralists railed against prostitution and as fears around sexually transmitted diseases like syphilis grew. Some believed that bathing itself was unhealthy, opening the pores in the skin in ways that could be dangerous. There were alternatives, of course. Benjamin Franklin described his practice of starting the morning with up to an hour of naked reading or writing as an "air bath." The German doctor Christian Franz Paullini published *Healing Filth Pharmacy* in 1694, encouraging use of human and animal feces and urine to protect and cure; it drew on rural and classical traditions of "manure therapies" and the fact that he wrote in the vernacular shows he intended it for popular audiences. Whether they used it is hard to tell, but it was republished often (Ward 2019).

Many Europeans thought that changing underclothes more frequently was all they needed to do to preserve hygiene. Linen was the more important second skin that merged propriety and cleanliness, and they claimed that Africans and Native Americans who preferred regular bathing in place of regularly changed underclothes were the truly unclean ones (Brown 2009; Ward 2019). European disdain for bathing was in part a fear of nudity. Underclothes rather than clean skin became the carriers of hygiene and civility, with particularly complex gender codes. Schools, books of manners, and enclosures for children and adults drilled the use of linens as the necessary first covering of a healthy body. It began with swaddling, with infants wrapped tightly in lengths of cloth to prevent them from harming themselves and help their bones grow straight. The process was so time-consuming that swaddling clothes might be changed rarely, making the dirt and smell even more powerful. Nonetheless, to forgo linens was to be naked and dirty, no matter what your age or the state of

Figure 11 Men bathing in the Arno. Jacques Callot, 1621 (Rijksmuseum)

your body or mind. This was projected on to women above all, and menstrual cloths came to be considered vital (Read 2013; McClive 2016). Bathing would return by the end of the early modern period, with bathhouses and spas multiplying through the eighteenth century and fads for sea baths and river bathing (see Figure 11). Yet these were seen as exceptional and medical, and not central to a regular – let alone frequent – regime of personal hygiene. Bathing remained rigorously divided by class and gender and turned into a highly private exercise, while linens remained the more important tools of hygiene and civilization. Only in the nineteenth century did a culture of bathing spread rapidly among the middle classes. In a weirdly ironic reversal it became associated with colonial racialization, as Jews, Asians, and Indigenous people were regularly dismissed as "dirty," "smelly," and "uncivilized" (Brown 2009; Ward 2019).

4.3 Smells of Profit

The sites of colonialism – warehouses, ships, plantations, walled compounds – carried a wide range of smells that fixed and transported memory and emotion. The enormous warehouses of the Dutch East India Company (VOC) in Amsterdam were redolent with scents of nutmeg, mace, cloves, and coffee. With extensive support of the Dutch Republic, the monopoly VOC pioneered forms of financing, shipping, and military support that others quickly imitated.

Its factors smuggled coffee plants from Yemen, burned nutmeg groves they couldn't control in Indonesia, invaded and seized settlements in Jakarta and Ambon, and fought English and Portuguese competitors across Asia. The English, French, Swedish, and Danish East India companies provided competition, but the VOC continued to trade within and beyond Asia on an order of magnitude far beyond any of them until its decline and bankruptcy at the end of the eighteenth century.

The fortunes that the VOC fueled can be seen in the rows of palatial homes lining the canals that Amsterdam dug in new circuits as the ships arrived from Indonesia. It is immortalized in the Turkish carpets, blue and white ceramic ware, and tobacco pipes crowding the still lives that merchants and artisans hung on their freshly plastered walls alongside tavern scenes, Asiatic landscapes, and maps of home and colonies (Alpers 1983; Chong 1987; Klaver 2014). With their maps, paintings, Delft blue ceramics, and pipes, the Dutch turned a foreign empire into an extension of their domestic spaces. Perhaps more than the sight of those goods or the feel of the textiles, what most domesticated what they considered "their" Spice Islands was the scent and taste of nutmeg, mace, cumin, cloves, and ginger. A culture raised on gruel, bread, and butter packed these aromatic spices into cheese, folded them into baking, and stirred them into soups and stews. And fixed them in memory. The scent of spice cakes was the smell of memory and dreams – in this case, of empire and of home, an odor of profit, mission, and destiny in which they took both religious and commercial pride. Global exchanges transformed diets everywhere, but scent was a primary way that Europeans inhaled and possessed the world. The key to the VOC's enormous profits lay not only in its financial techniques and military ruthlessness, but in its ability to create consumer markets that had never existed before. Like the paintings on a shoemaker's wall, spices went from being an indulgence of the rich to an affordable and often seasonal luxury for ordinary artisans, merchants, and workers, particularly when combined with other colonial commodities like sugar, tea, and coffee. The Dutch, Swedish, Danish, French, and English East India monopoly companies loaded spices into enormous warehouses in Amsterdam, Gothenburg, Copenhagen, Nantes, and London. They shipped them to shops and landed ginger, cloves, and nutmeg in kitchens across Northern Europe that had rarely held such an abundance of powerfully aromatic ingredients (Brook 2007).

These spices had nowhere near the same impact in southern Europe, where wider ranges of herbs and seasonings had long shaped the smell and taste of food. Yet the spice trade was critical in Manila too, with a formidable trade in camphor and benzoin, both derived from the bark or resin of trees and prized for their medical properties. Travelers wrote that Manila was redolent with the smell of both, which were brought by traders from Japan, Taiwan, and Sumatra. Stored in volume, they announced their presence in any shops and warehouses that distributed them. When marketed out of Manila to other parts of Asia, Mexico, or Europe, they were burned in smaller amounts as a form of incense used medically for fumigation. Sprinkling small amounts on live coals would release the scent, which could either be inhaled or directed to parts of the body needing cure. Perfumers prized benzoin in particular and integrated it into the scents they manufactured for personal use. Manila's cosmopolitan residents were famous for their use of perfume among a host of luxuries that traded in the port. As a destination for thousands of traders the city itself was as crowded, unsanitary, and unhygienic as any other global entrepôt in the period, becoming even more so in the intense heat of summer. No doubt because of this many of the Tagalog, Chinese, and Japanese living there bathed frequently, dressed in light silks and linens, and wore fragrant oils and exquisite fragrances derived from plants, animals (musk, ambergris, civet), and tree resins like benzoin. They traded all of these and produced and exported Manila Elemi, an aromatic resin like fennel and mace (Reyes 2017).

Colonialism's odors were more limited in Boston. It had an extensive reach across the Americas and to England as the hub of broad trading networks that extended through the Caribbean. Spices and medicines came through its shops, yet the commodities that it warehoused and traded in bulk were far less exotic or aromatic. With land on Barbados and Jamaica at a premium for plantation crops, Bostonians provided much of the diet that fed these islands' enslaved and indentured workers. Flour and vegetables were hardly the stuff of Proustian memories, and sheep and cattle let off odors that may have stirred memories but hardly fed dreams. Fish were among the items landed and then reshipped from Boston in large volumes, but much of it was relatively odorless dried salt cod. What Boston received in trade was sugar and rum, which were highly valuable though less aromatic than cloves, camphor, or musk (Landon 1996; Bowen 1998; Cheek 1998).

Spices and foodstuffs generated only some of the smells of colonialism, that part where consumers bought the goods that merchants had sourced and shipped. They less often smelled the odors of producing those goods or securing the labor force for the plantation economies necessary for the raw materials. At the end of our period the West African Olaudah Equiano (1745–97), also known as Gustavas Vassa, wrote of the experience of being enslaved and transported as a steady intensification of filth and stink. It began with hygiene that became more slack as he was kidnapped and marched at age 11 from Benin to the coast. It continued to the "pestilential stench" of human waste and dead bodies in the airless hold of the ship that took him over the Atlantic to Barbados and Virginia

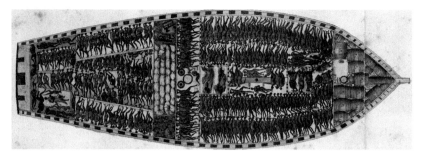

Figure 12 Slave deck of French ship. Anon, 1770 (Wikimedia Commons)

before sale to a Royal Navy lieutenant (see Figure 12). Sold twice more, he narrowly escaped plantation service but worked and traded on Atlantic ships, possibly landing periodically in Boston, before buying his freedom. Equiano reclaimed his Ibo name in his best-selling 1789 autobiography, which became a powerful work in the abolitionist movement thanks in part to his ability to evoke the full sensory register of enslavement (Brown 2009). Sensory evocations played powerfully on European imaginations, generating horror and outrage, while the legal discussions or financial realities that implicated them more directly in the mechanics of enslavement were kept abstract and distant. Equiano's abolitionist "owners" were happy to release him, but only after he had reimbursed their investment.

4.4 Purifying Smells

Those enjoying the scents of spices in shops or baking in Amsterdam or Boston might not think of the extent to which plantation enslavement was the human cost of these rich aromas. Amsterdam's artists painted plantation landscapes, but these were usually as placid as a conventional Dutch landscape, minus the towering clouds and with only distinct vegetation and colonial architecture to indicate a location outside Batavia rather than Delft. Humans were rare and tiny presences in these landscapes. While colonial portraitists might paint one or two black enslaved into household gatherings, the hundreds kept under the plantation owners' control whose work paid the painter went unrecorded. The "pestilential stench" in the hold of a slave ship was handled by those on the top deck with small vials of perfume that they could hold to their noses when the smell of shit, sickness, and death became overwhelming. Mobilizing smells to counter hard realities was a long tradition brought into play most often in enclosed and liminal spaces where they could refocus attention from immediate inconveniences to future rewards.

The exotic aromas of frankincense used in church services had obscured the smell of bodies decaying under the pavement. Before the spice ships sailed, large caravans had moved tons of incense overland from the Arabian peninsula into Europe to feed the demand (Le Mageur 2015). It's perhaps no coincidence that Protestants ceased burying bodies in their churches in large numbers around the time that they ceased using incense in worship. Clear air, like the clear words of a preacher's sermon or a congregation's metric psalm, and the clear light streaming in from windows without stained glass were part of the sensory package of the new confession observed in Amsterdam or Boston. Protestants held to the transparency of God's Word – even as they fought fiercely over the interpretations and implications of biblical texts. Frankincense and myrrh continued to smolder in churches in Florence, Manila, and across the Catholic world, where they were not only purging earthly decay but promising the sweeter future of heaven; Catholics, Buddhists, Jews, and Muslims all considered incense to be an olfactory and visual form of prayer, purification, and devotion. The clouds of incense pouring out of censors swung in Catholic worship anticipated the aromas of heaven. Using it was not just an act of displacement, like taking a vial of perfume to your nose in a stinking slave ship. Incense challenged the Devil's signature scents: the rotten egg smell of sulfur that spoke to hell's location deep under the earth or the newer scent of skunks that amazed and appalled European settlers in North America. French settlers and missionaries in Quebec thought that skunks carried Lucifer's maleficent odor, one describing it as a "symbol of sin . . . no sewer ever smelled so bad." (Le Jeune 1635). This convinced some of the Devil's stronger sway around Indigenous communities in particular. Frankincense and myrrh signaled the new heaven and new earth that Jesus promised.

This came out powerfully in the conviction that the bodies of saints did not suffer corruption after death. They might decay, but the fumes of decomposition did not emanate from the corpses of those translated directly to heaven. Among the changes transforming the Catholic Church as it globalized in the period of religious reformation was a new and more rigorous procedure for determining sanctity. When a charismatic religious leader or a holy woman died, had they moved immediately to join the saints in heaven and advocate for those on earth? It had long been up to local communities to determine this, making saints' cults among the most localized and potentially random elements in Catholic spirituality. Protestant mockery put a halt to saint-making for almost a century. When finally revived, it came with a complex set of legal procedures to weigh evidence of miracles and bureaucratic tribunals of review with the pope as the ultimate arbiter. This certainly limited any popular canonizations on distant mission fields, and indeed the saints canonized from the seventeenth century were largely those who had the money, expertise, and patience of religious orders or state governments to promote them: males, clerics, Europeans (Burke 1984; Ditchfield 1992).

Figure 13 Woman smoking. Cornelis Bega, 17th century (National Gallery of Art, Washington)

One earlier test that remained was olfactory: a stinking corpse was no friend of God. The odor of sanctity was sweet, mysterious, and compelling. It was the pervasive odor of piety, the miraculous aroma of purification, the scent of the better future promised to those entering worship spaces already redolent of frankincense and myrrh (Benoit 2012).

Those focused on earthy pleasure could get much of the same thing from tobacco (see Figure 13). Indigenous people in the Americas had certainly used tobacco and sweetgrass in spiritual rituals, but it never gained that association for colonial travelers. Tobacco reached West Africa from eastern North America by the late sixteenth century, being put into distinctively designed clay pipes that had made their way from Asia and Arabia centuries before, and that enslaved Africans would then bring with them to the Americas (Philips 1983; Bagley 2021). For some tobacco was the smell of community and conviviality, associations front and center among First Nations who used it in ceremonies of welcome and purification. While Indigenous women and children participated in these ceremonies, tobacco usually signaled male sociability in Europe, where smoking became a marker of masculine adulthood and female gender-bending. Europeans also translated the idea of purification into their own biological science of the humors and recommended the astringent odor of burning tobacco as way of drying a body thrown out of balance by too many of the phlegmatic humors that dominated the female constitution. "Medical smoking" was remedial more than convivial, a bodily cure much like fumigation with camphor and benzine but delivered more individually and directly through a pipe. For others burning tobacco was the devil's stench, an association they again used to denigrate Indigenous culture. Whatever the associations, tobacco quickly became another of the scents whose early modern demand sent seeds and plants across continents, propelled the creation of plantations worked by enslaved laborers, and generated global trading networks and fortunes. Thanks perhaps to nicotine, it survived long beyond the demise of belief in bodily humors. The smell of tobacco became a signature of adult men and sometimes women, associated with the community and conviviality that Indigenous people had valued.

5 The Taste of Time

Eating patterns followed the rhythms of ritual, festive, and seasonal calendars. The health of foods and imperatives of diets were often determined less by nutritional qualities than by considerations of class, age, gender, race, seasons, and solar and lunar cycles. The Catholic calendars of Florence and Manila shaped diet differently than the Protestant calendars of Amsterdam and Boston, and there were exceptions to religious rules found in each. Some emphasized what you could or should *not* eat, while the exchange of plants and animals in global trade movements multiplied the availability of "new" foods. Consumers in different parts of the world responded quite differently to new staples, luxuries, and drugs. Chocolate and peppers were adopted relatively quickly; potatoes and tomatoes only after a century or two. How did Florentines and Amsterdammers respond differently to these expanding tables and how did consumers in Boston and Manila bring together the taste of local foods and colonial imports? How were changing tastes the product of marketing by monopoly companies that established plantations worked by enslaved laborers on an industrial scale around the globe?

5.1 Global Foodways

Manilans greeted the Mexican galleys arriving annually from Acapulco for more than just their loads of silver bars and coins. The ships' holds carried tobacco and chocolate as well, and these cargoes were likely moved quickly along the streets as they made their way from the port and into the city's markets and mouths. The Mexican ships arrived less predictably than the junks sailing from Fujian in China during the May to July window determined by seasonal monsoons. Once again, the crowds greeting them on the wharves along the Pasig river weren't just anticipating handling the bolts of silk in their holds. They looked forward to fresh vegetables from Fujian and tuna and wheat flour from Japan. Whether it was with luxuries like tobacco and chocolate, staples like maize and pork, or newly exchanged items like chili peppers, the Asian and European expatriate communities settled around Manila turned it into an intersection of cultural foodways. Shared techniques and tastes flowed into each other and then shaped the culinary currents that returned to their home metropoles.

With the schedules of fleets set by winds and storms, the fresh foods shipped from distant places into an entrepôt like Manila naturally set a temporal rhythm to eating. Foods that were preserved were less subject to this, and the chocolate on Mexican galleys could last longer before spoiling, which was an advantage for a voyage that regularly took many months. Ships sailing the far shorter distance from Fujian had far more perishable fresh food on them, and far larger markets in Manila to justify loading them up for the trip. Settlers, farmers, and merchants aimed to see if transplants could replace transports, but some crops resisted adaptation. Catholic worship drove demand for flour – for eucharistic hosts – and wine. Neither wheat nor grapes flourished in the Luzon peninsula, so Spanish nuns and priests were as keen as Japanese traders for the wheat shipped from Nagasaki. Their efforts to reciprocate were less successful, as time worked against them: two barrels of wine that had already spent two years in transit from Lisbon before being forwarded to Nagasaki likely arrived there as vinegar (Tremml-Warner 2015; Reyes 2017).

More food moved further around the early modern world and in more ways than we might imagine (Krondl 2013; see Figure 14). Some early foodways transported the familiar to keep memories of home at the table of those who had migrated, like the wheat noodles for Japanese merchants in Manila. Some moved familiar staples in shorter circuits driven by demand. For all the VOC

Figure 14 Portuguese ship in Nagasaki. Anon, c. 1625 (Rijksmuseum)

ships arriving into Amsterdam's harbor with cloves, nutmeg, and mace, an even greater number brought loads of herring from the Baltic to feed demand from consumers across North Europe. Southern Baltic herring spawned in the spring, making late spring and early summer the prime season for eating them fresh. Amsterdam's shipbuilders developed early forms of factory ships that could process catches on the water and so stay out for longer periods and bring back larger cargoes; salting, smoking, and preserving in vinegar extended the times for eating herring. Baltic freighters also began moving wheat to Mediterranean cities like Florence in the 1590s when famines followed the collapse of local supply. Amsterdam was again the pivot in a trade that emptied Nordic warehouses of grain once navigation was possible in the spring, and then carried on through summer. Amsterdam merchant and mayor Cornelis Hooft brokered the first shipment of rye in October 1591 and actively pushed to expand the new trade by sending one of his sons to Italy to learn the language and manage local contracts (Van Tielhof 2002).

While mass hunger fed this demand, Florence was also on the receiving end of more exotic cargoes. Grand Duke Francesco I imported many varieties of lemon trees planted into large clay pots located in the gardens around his city palace in summer and then brought into a purpose-built lemon house (*limonaia*) to shelter through the winter. The demand here was as much scientific as culinary – citrus from the Levant and southern Italy had long featured on elite tables further north. Expanding supply allowed Florentine cooks to be more inventive and adapting existing plants to the climate, and finding new cultivars brought the Grand Dukes both prestige and income – by the eighteenth century they had 116 varieties (Attlee, 2014). Paris's Jardin du Roi and London's Kew Gardens would soon take up the example planted at the Boboli, fed by the same mix of taste, scientific curiosity, and financial gain, with grander imperial ambition added as well.

Empires moved foods the furthest, and the most consequential shipments of plants and animals were part of the so-called Columbian Exchange (Crosby 1972). Ships sailing to and from Seville and Lisbon transformed the global diet, moving tomatoes, potatoes, peppers, corn, cassava, and legumes from the Americas to Europe and beyond and bringing wheat, vines, and apples to the Americas. William Blaxton planted the first apple orchard in North America in 1625 just outside of what would become Boston and a decade and a half later would breed the first American variety, Blaxton's Yellow Sweeting (Smith 1997). Exchanges of animals were as consequential if less evenly matched. Pigs, sheep, cattle, and horses would transform American landscapes as much as they reshaped its diets, particularly as these pasturing animals were moved into rural areas vacated by the collapse of American populations in the face of new European diseases and exploitation. The Columbian Exchange extended to diseases like smallpox, which cut like a scythe through Indigenous populations. Few animals traveled the other way, the turkey being perhaps the most notable if not a particularly widespread exception (Eiche 2004). It's not clear whether turkeys were among the wild fowl that early Pilgrims ate at Thanksgiving, though it was more likely that ducks and geese were on the table, together with venison.

Bostonians would come to make wild turkey part of their diet, but it did not become an iconic food for Thanksgiving – and indeed, Thanksgiving itself wasn't widely adopted – until the mid-nineteenth century. Boston was the doorway for one of four dominant foodways coming out of England to America, and its largely East Anglian population ate relatively little wild food and even a narrower range of fish compared to the south and west English migrants who had settled in Virginia and the Carolinas. Archaeological studies of privies show that the latter ate three times the variety of fish and seafood that Bostonians did and employed home-country methods like frying and fricasseeing that would define southern American foodways. New Englanders preferred farm-raised livestock over wild animals, usually boiled and baked their food rather than frying it, and used few spices (Landon 1996; Bowen 1998; Cheek 1998; Bagley 2021).

Migration bent foodways in unpredictable ways. Need, custom, and cultural expectations shaped whether, when, and how new and old foods were eaten (see Figure 15). When Flemish settlers brought their Holstein and Frisian cows to the Azores in the 1470s, they planted cultures of cheesemaking that continue today in wheels of São Jorge cheese that look and taste much like Dutch gouda and edam. When Bostonians exported lamb, dried cod, livestock, and vegetables to the Caribbean, the populations of enslaved Africans who received them bent the hybrid of East Anglian and American foods yet further with their own spices and methods of preparation. While seeds and plants often moved quickly along trade routes, the unfamiliar foods they generated often took far longer to make it on to tables and into diets. As thousands of merchants and artisans from complex food cultures converged around Manila, they couldn't help but sample food across cultural boundaries and begin integrating spices, vegetables, and techniques into their own cooking. Chinese cooks in Manila seem to have picked up on chili peppers from local cooks and on confections of sugar, butter, and eggs from the Spanish. Tagalog cooks taught the mix of sour and sweet tastes while Spanish shared cured beef and pork and frying in oil. Maize, tomatoes, and chocolate came to the area from the Americas while Meishan pigs moved from China to early modern Europe to be bred with local stock that were larger but less fertile, creating new breeds like Yorkshire and Landraces (Tremml-Warner 2015; Reyes 2017).

The dynamic was similar to what had happened centuries earlier when European crusaders returned from the Levant, bringing a memory of and demand for what they had eaten there, to the enormous financial benefit of the Italian merchants who

Figure 15 Market stall Batavia. Andries Beekman, c. 1666 (Rijksmuseum)

filled that demand. While medieval merchants had traded rare foods and spices that could not be raised in Europe's colder climates, their early modern counterparts also moved plants and animals for planting, breeding, and domestication. Sheer necessity and the example of Indigenous co-cultivation of the "three sisters" corn, beans, and squash put these vegetables on Boston tables. Yet they didn't make a deep impact on migrants' diets and so were slower to make their way back to England, even though many of the early settlers did return within a few decades. Seeds and plants were easy to export, but the culinary example of these and other American foods was slow to take root overseas. America's peppers quickly moved into European kitchens; tomatoes took decades and potatoes at least a century and a half (Krondl 2013). And while colonizing powers did much of the moving, Europe was not the inevitable hub of their exchanges. A VOC trader stole coffee plants from Mocha in Yemen in 1616 and the company tried unsuccessfully to root them in the Netherlands before sending them to Sri Lanka in 1658 and then Java in 1696, where climate and plantation cultivation turned it into one of the company's most valuable signature commodities (Prendergast 2019).

5.2 Early Modern Food Rules – Eating by Time, Space, Faith, and Constitution

It wasn't just unfamiliar tastes and conservative palates that delayed Europeans from accepting "new" foods like potatoes and tomatoes and introducing them to their kitchens and tables. They had complex rules that calculated the impact of foods on an individual's balance of humors and ranked them by class and gender (see Figure 16). When an upper-class woman resisted wheaten bread, or a peasant

Figure 16 Banquet piece with mince pie. William Claesz Heda, 1635 (National Gallery of Art, Washington)

ate chickpeas, they were following the dictates of contemporary biology, gender norms, and class boundaries. Foods generated bodily heat and fluids regardless of the temperature they were served at or any liquid used in preparation. Before tasting anything, you needed to assess your condition and plans. A Florentine humanist applied the rules to determine that the best time for an elite couple to conceive a child was an hour or so after a meal on a warm May evening, when taste, food, and setting combined to create the most fertile emotional and physical conditions; according to the science of the day, procreation required pleasure. A smart eater in Florence knew her or his own constitution, judged the season and time of day, and ate accordingly (Bell 1999; Grieco, 2020). To do otherwise was to risk falling desperately ill, so trying new foods was a potentially dangerous experiment. Enough people risked that experiment over time to change the diets of their regions: potatoes transformed eating in Ireland, India, and Germany, tomatoes and peppers became the mainstay of Italian cooking, cassava became a staple across South Saharan Africa, and pork and beef became centerpieces of Mexican and central American diets.

Religious confessions added a further layer of rules around foods and eating (Friedenreich 2015; Kissane 2018). These established regimes of purification, discipline, and identity around when and what to eat, or whether to eat at all. Fasting accentuated taste. What made fast days memorable was not only the days or weeks of not tasting certain foods – or not eating at all – but the feasts that broke or bracketed the fasts. Muslims observing the month of Ramadan ate and drank nothing during the day, but at nightfall they ate communal *iftar* meals featuring dates and other sweets. Jews ate a large festive meal on the eve of Yom Kippur because the day of repentance itself required fasting. Early Christians had continued some Jewish fast days (e.g., Wednesday or Friday) in the form of the Black Fast, which meant eating one meal a day after sundown without meat, eggs, or dairy. Catholics extended this fasting through the forty-day period of Lent to heighten the sense of reflection and repentance for the sins that Christ had taken on himself in his crucifixion that followed, but they bracketed fasting with feasting. The festive week of Carnival could be a riot of feasting that prepared them for the coming period when they set meat aside (*carne-vale*), culminating in Fat Tuesday (*Mardi-gras*), when they used up any animal fats in cooking before starting the fast on Ash Wednesday. Eggs, sweets, and meat returned to their tables on Easter Sunday to celebrate the crucified Christ's return to life. Followers of all the Abrahamic traditions used temporal rhythms of fasting and feasting to mark their highest holy days. Children and converts became aware of faith traditions through food first of all: the first taste of a date, an egg, or a piece of lamb before or after a fast likely made a more immediate and powerful impression than a sermon. Yet it was all of a piece. Alternating the times of abstinence and festive eating turned the dynamics of spiritual repentance and celebratory thankfulness into a powerful sensory experience taking place around a family dining table.

It wasn't just when you ate, but what. Together with the times of fasting and feasting, there were forbidden foods. Pork was the fundamental divide: neither Jews nor Muslims could taste it, but it was a staple of many Christian diets, not least because pigs were small, cheap, and easy to raise and their meat was easily preserved. As a result, eating pork took on significance far beyond taste. In Spain, Portugal, and Italy, Catholic inquisitors found it a convenient marker for identifying *conversos* and *moriscos* who had converted from Judaism and Islam respectively but maintained their ancestral dietary and hygienic rules. This made neighbors suspicious, and when inquisitors asked these neighbors about converts' religious practices, they got answers that were more often about food and drink than about theology (Campbell 2017; Cassen 2018). With pork a key marker and sausage the most popular way of eating it, Portuguese Jews and conversos developed *alheira* sausages made with chicken, herbs, and bread filling to hide their avoidance of pork. Jews in the ghettos of Florence or Rome were freer to keep the dietary rules (*kashrut*), but their butchers faced further complications since not all cuts were kosher. They had to be careful to remove the fat and all traces of the sciatic nerve and couldn't use a whole carcass, so they had to collaborate with gentile butchers or find ways to sell to gentile clients (Stow 2024). The single butcher serving Florence's ghetto had the only shop with doors leading both into the ghetto and out to the city market just outside it.

As religious reforms spawned divisions through the sixteenth century, there was no clearer sign of Catholicism's origin as a Mediterranean religion than the meatless days that filled its liturgical calendar. Beyond the season of Lent there were other religious holidays and "Fish Fridays," and some Catholics observed Wednesday and Saturday fasts as well. Serious Catholics might spend over half the year avoiding meat. In ports like Manila and Amsterdam before its "Alteration," these could easily be fish days. Yet the cost of fresh fish mounted quickly as you moved inland, and even in a riverine city like Florence or Paris it could be many times the price of meat. The late sixteenth-century account books of the Earls of Derby show them spending 20 pence for a fresh cod and 2 pence for a chicken (Raines 1853). Salted fish was an alternative, putting both herring and cod on tables far from the Baltic and Atlantic where they were caught. Other tastes were limited. Abundant vegetables and legumes could fill up Catholic tables in southern Europe, but as you moved further north into areas with shorter growing seasons there were fewer vegetables in fewer varieties available. These were areas long accustomed to eating meat instead. Many did not care for the taste of fish and were happy to find excuses for avoiding it (Campbell 2017). Some Catholics circumvented dietary rules by pleading special circumstances like poor health that required some animal protein, or paying to buy a "butter permit." As with Jewish and Muslim converts, what you ate or avoided sent a strong and public message. When a group of radical religious reformers emerged in Zurich and began a rapid spread across Europe from the 1520s, their two most controversial public actions challenging Catholicism were giving each other a second baptism in the Rhine River and eating pork sausages in Lent. Protestants who couldn't agree on much apart from their aversion to Catholicism almost universally abandoned the dietary rules that had banned meat, eggs, cheese, and butter in Lent, on Fridays, and at other times of the year. They derided these rituals, and indeed almost any Catholic religious ritual practices, as "Jewish," which was ironic considering how closely the Catholic Inquisition monitored the tables of Jewish and Muslim converts. The Protestant God was omnivorous, and it was within the freedom of the Christian to eat any meat whenever they liked (Albala 2011; Kissane 2018).

5.3 Poor Diets

Some people barely ate at all. Apart from customs, rules, and foodways that preserved traditional habits, poverty kept many from eating more than a few basic starches. Amsterdam's merchants could bring in all the herring and spices they wanted, but most people kept to a diet of oatmeal gruel taken once or twice a day. Parisian laborers ate as much as kilogram of bread a day in the seventeenth century and even more a century later. Frescoes and account books show that bread was also the staple in charitable enclosures for orphans and beggars like Florence's Innocenti, London's Bridewell, and Amsterdam's Almoners' Orphanage. Notably, the orphans sheltering in the city's Citizen Orphanage received a significantly better diet, including animal protein and vegetables, because it was thought that these children should be trained to eat the diet of their class (McCants 1997). For paupers in Italian institutions, any vegetables and soups that accompanied the staple were called *companatico* or "something to eat with bread." Poor Bostonians had more protein among their options, and judging again from their privies, it seems that poverty led some to eat wild food that they caught. The sedimentary layers of Katherine Nanny Naylor's privy show how the family diet declined after she was granted the first divorce in Massachusetts in 1671 and her abusive and adulterous husband Edward was banished, leaving her to raise four children. While still far better off than most Bostonians, Katherine and her children now began eating more deer, pigeon, ducks, geese, and lobster (Bagley 2021). Their situation demonstrated how poverty could rise and fall at different stages in the life cycle. Other factors entered in. Some of those eating wild food further south in Virginia and the Carolinas may have been following traditions imported along foodways from the west and south of England, but many more were likely dealing with poverty and higher rates of enslavement (Cheek 1998).

Religious traditions that emphasized fasting on holy days connected it to being generous with gifts of food to the poor. During Ramadan Muslims increased their giving of *zakat*, the alms that supported soup kitchens and household donations of bread; Yom Kippur was similarly a focus for Jewish charity (Fitzpatrick 2013; Campbell 2017). In the middle of Lent the administrators of Bologna's civic charity collected alms and food and set out special meals for the poor. Even the poor deserved a good time occasionally, when they might taste what the wealthy took for granted. For most, though, bread was a common symbol and reality of poverty. Frequently baked with adulterated grains or cut with roots, seeds, and other plants, it was nonetheless the key staple for most Europeans. Hospitals distributed loaves to paupers and pilgrims at the door; in Florence, the main hospital also offered chicken soup. Innovative remedies for poverty inevitably began with and revolved around bread. When authorities and philanthropists in Bologna developed interlocking social systems for alleviating poverty, these included centralized weekly distribution of bread from four centers to designated recipients, increased imports of rye from the Baltic, higher taxes charged for the privilege of baking white bread, and a fund to buy and stockpile wheat in times of plenty so that it could be sold at below-market prices during times of famine (Terpstra 2013). Boston developed a similar scheme to handle seasonal price fluctuations and make wheat more affordable in the winter (Peterson 2019).

Charging a higher tax on white bread points to how older convictions around the humors shaped consumption of even this staple. Upper-class consumers had more delicate constitutions that left them unable to digest darker and unrefined flours. "Pumpernickel" translates as "farting devil" and this Germanic and Central European staple was notorious for generating gases. The account book of English knight William Petre shows that he served three types of bread in his household: a lighter-tasting white for his own family, a mixed grain "yeoman's bread" for the better servants working in the house, and a heavy, dark, and meaty "carter's loaf" for those laboring in the fields. His selection wasn't just about class but also reflected what medical authorities thought the distinct constitutions of elites, domestic servants, and farm laborers required in order to do their daily work. Eating outside your class, gender, and age could be dangerous. Tasting foods meant for others on the social ladder could breed unrest – an Italian proverb cautioned "do not let the peasant know how good cheese is with pears" because they might use violence to get this elite luxury. Yet it could also be a calculated gamble: some upper-class diners thought that since peasants were almost like animals, tasting peasant foods like garlic, root vegetables, and beans from time to time might give them a peasant's animalistic sexual potency (Montanari 2010; Grieco 2020). Many of the poor could only dream of anything beyond these rough foods. Popular songs and stories fed common legends about a utopian paradise that Bostonians would have heard called *Cockaigne*, Florentines *Cuccagna*, Amsterdammers *Luilekkerland*, and Manila's Spaniards *Jauja* or *cucaña* (see Figure 17). In all these mythical paradises sausages hung from trees, wine ran in fountains, and sweets abounded. Carnival floats and public festivals picked up the legend and savvy officials knew that one way to forestall revolt was to occasionally make it a reality, being sure to take the credit as the benevolent providers of abundance (Reed 2015). That was the thinking when Bologna's authorities marked the feast day of St Bartholomew (August 24) by tipping a huge roast pig off a balcony on the communal palace, to be ripped apart and devoured on the spot by waiting crowds below. They even added a soup course, poured directly on to the crowd.

The Italian proverb about cheese and pears foregrounds taste as it combines two foods that exemplified lower- and upper-class diets through the medieval and

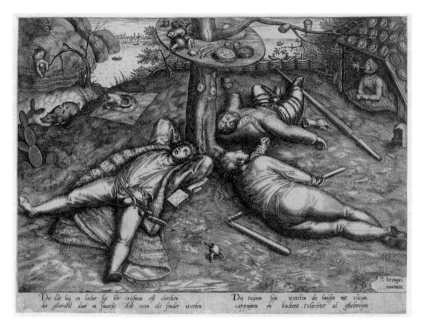

Figure 17 Luilekkerland. Pieter van der Heyden, c. 1600 (Rijksmuseum)

early modern periods. Cheese was the cheap protein of the lower classes. It gained a foothold in upper-class diets in part through the need of monks and friars to find some way of getting protein while observing frequent meatless fast days. This was why many of the distinctive varieties of cheeses produced across Europe, and particularly in France, originated in monasteries. Pears, like all tree fruits, were seen as the preserve of the upper classes. One characteristic that gave pears their special class appeal was the fact that they spoiled so quickly. While the sheer durability of cheese added to its value as a lower-class food, only the truly wealthy could afford to cultivate, eat, and give tender pears as gifts. And while even cheese that was shot through with mold could find its place at the table, a rotten pear was best discarded no matter how much it had cost. Traditional knowledge attributed to both cheese and pears the quality of closing off the stomach and so aiding digestion and improving the humors. With cheese and pears both finding their places at the end of peasant and patrician meals respectively, it was only a matter of time before some transgressive diners would combine them and through taste realize what a wonderful pairing they made.

5.4 Affordable Luxuries at Incalculable Cost

Luxury foods like chocolate and coffee moved far more quickly along early modern global foodways than potatoes or corn. They moved even faster when used in combinations. Spices might have had much less impact had they not been adopted together with sugar, which moved most quickly across the globe and had the greatest impact. It certainly made chocolate, coffee, and tea more palatable. Originating in Arabia, sugar was cultivated for centuries in such small quantities that it remained a highly prized and highly expensive luxury that posed little competition to other natural sweeteners like honey. Medieval Europeans used it sparingly and often chiefly for medical purposes, either to balance humors, prepare syrups, or make unpleasant tasting medicines more palatable. The time to taste sugar was when you were ill, and while some religious authorities feared that it was a fast-breaker, few doctors encountered resistance from patients when prescribing it for fevers, constipation, or depression (Mintz 1985).

Changes in the scale of cultivation emerged as the first plantations were developed in mid-Atlantic islands, yet another example of plants moving around the world in the early modern period as merchants aimed to feed demand (see Figure 18). By the sixteenth century some capitalists were seeing the potential profits of ramped up production, but the work was hard, particularly in those equatorial areas where sugar cane grew best. Forced labor with Indigenous peoples soon collapsed along with their populations, and the Atlantic triangle of enslavement began expanding to fill the gap. Ships from Nantes, Bristol, Lisbon, Seville, and Amsterdam brought cargoes to trade in West African forts for enslaved men, women, and children who were then carried in the holds on the

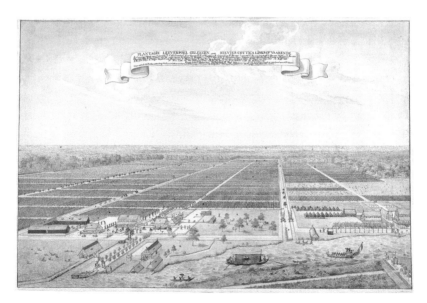

Figure 18 Suriname coffee plantation. Anon, 18th century (Rijksmuseum)

Middle Passage to the Americas to become chattel labor on newly expanding plantations. These ships then returned to Europe with the commodities produced on the plantations worked by those same enslaved. Sweetness and power transformed the global economy within decades as brokers in Amsterdam, London, and Seville realized how sugar could increase demand for other commodities like spices, chocolate, tea, and coffee (Mintz 1985).

Preparing these luxuries in colonial sites or metropolitan factories involved boiling, drying, grinding, and roasting. These industrial processes rendered spices, sugar, coffee, and tea less perishable and easier to transport, and this profoundly altered the effect of time on taste. What had been a rare taste enjoyed by a few and limited perhaps to a particular festive season like Christmas became an affordable luxury consumed weekly or even daily at set times or with certain meals. Markets expanded as costs fell and volumes rose, changing fundamentally the foodways of ever larger groups of consumers and domesticating once exotic and foreign foodstuffs. As we noted earlier, Amsterdammers began flavoring their cheese with cumin and cloves. Bakers across northern Europe folded ginger, cinnamon, nutmeg, and cardamon into cakes and cookies. Coffee houses first appeared in Damascus after the Ottomans took over Yemen, moving to Istanbul by 1555, and opening a century later in London (1652), Paris (1672), and Vienna (1685). The first one in America opened in Boston in 1676. A British traveler who encountered coffee in Turkey in 1610 described it as "blacke as soot and tasting not much unlike it," adding however that it helped digestion and drinking it sharpened the senses (Prendergast 2019, 7–8). An Amsterdam artisan writing in the 1680s noted that while coffee houses had been rare four decades earlier, now they were always stuffed with customers. Spaces for coffee, tea, and chocolate offered the familiarity of taverns without the drunkenness and generated a whole new range of places to visit at different times of the day to carry out business, play games like backgammon and chess, and talk about politics and current events. Their sociability is celebrated in some circles as having fostered a middle-class political culture, but most excluded women, laborers, and the poor. Caffeine also fed the needs of Torah students in the Venetian ghetto, as coffee allowed them to study and discuss scriptures long into the night after days spent working (Horowitz 1989; Cowan 2011).

A common element drew together all these affordable luxuries and the new foodways they were mapping: all were plantation crops, most relied on enslaved and forced labor, and most involved heavy capital investments far outside of Europe. Plantation production moved luxuries beyond aristocratic tables and made them affordable. Creating the consumer economy required the methods and marketing of brokers like the host of monopoly East India Companies multiplying across Europe. These privately owned joint-stock operations relied fundamentally on direct and indirect state support to provide the capital, military clout, and colonial infrastructure that made possible both the plantations where these commodities were produced and the enslavement and indenturing of the laborers working on them. Early modern colonialism was a deeply commercial enterprise, focused on creating and serving markets and shaped by and shaping the tastes of consumers.

6 The Times of Touch

When to touch and when not? Birth and death were both times of intense touch. The touch of the hand for love and healing contrasts to the touch of the lash (or indeed the hand again) for discipline and corporal punishment. The contaminating touch of a leper, the empowering touch of a relic, and the thaumaturgic touch of a king imbued touch with power and uncertainty. Offering or withholding touch might sometimes be counterintuitive: those involved in execution rituals might offer touch to comfort those about to die, while parents might withhold touch as part of the advice offered in both Protestant and Catholic manuals for how to shape those being taught how to live. The law implied touch in using the hand as a metaphor for control, and some who were empowered with that hand exercised the full measure of their authority through sexual and punitive touching. There were some areas of casual touch that we might not expect, like shared pots, plates, and glasses at a dining table, and many areas of forbidden touch between genders, ages, races, and social orders that might surprise us. Vision was a form of touch and might be counseled (gazing on spiritual objects) or forbidden (looking directly at the king). There were numerous prohibitions on touch, and enclosures both architectural and legal aimed to channel and prevent touching that might encourage bonds that authorities were determined to prevent.

6.1 The Hand

In the instructions it gives to the confraternity brothers who are going to comfort men condemned to death, a manual used in Florence encourages them to touch the prisoner: to greet him by hand when entering the cell, to clasp him on the back when he despairs, to touch him on the chest when he takes final communion. Possibly a murderer, arsonist, or bandit highwayman, the man about to die was likely young and scared, originating from outside the city, and soon to be erased from the earth. In their effort to ensure that his soul might yet be saved, the comforters worked to persuade him that they were accepting him as their brother. They used the gentle touch of familiars to give meaning to their words in the prison cell, on the procession to the scaffold, and up to the point of death. Their touch ushered him in to communion and on to heaven (Terpstra 2008).

The touch of a hand could mean very different kinds of human connection. It's likely that a prisoner only hours from his death had more often felt it delivered with violence than with care. Manuals on raising children weren't using metaphors when they advocated that parents or guardians use a firm hand or rod. This was the hand as a sign of authority and governance. In domestic settings a father or mother was advised to use the hand in discipline but also love. A Florentine source used gendered stereotypes: a young boy could remain under his mother's soft touch till age 6, when he should transfer to the firmer hand of his father. This conventional and stereotypical advice merging touch and emotion appears in a wide range of cultures. Affectionate embraces and tender strokes were no less important than hands raised in punishment when it came to directing a child toward adulthood. Early modern instructions on raising children often used terms like "governance" and reached to botanical metaphors about training plants to grow straight and tall. Early Jesuits in Canada criticized First Nations people for being excessively indulgent and failing to discipline their children, claiming it bred insolence and laziness. Was it a backhanded way of acknowledging that it led to adults unimpressed with Jesuits and unlikely to follow their many rules and commands? The hand that pruned, grafted, and fed demonstrated attention and demanded obedience. What may have been harder than a hand raised in discipline was the absence of any hand at all. Anachronistically, perhaps, a modern-day London man abandoned to a foundling home and interviewed late in life spoke of it leaving him without knowing how to *live* with family. He regretted the effect on his own children – "my lost childhood and theirs"– because he'd never *felt* family life (Pugh 2007, 135).

Beyond physical touch, the hand was also a potent metaphor used in Roman law to denote authority. The authority or *potestas* of the father over a son or daughter or of a husband over a wife was symbolized by the hand, or *manus.* To be under someone's authority was to be "under their hand" and subject to their *mani*pulation. The hand gave food and clothes but might also carry a rod. This was the authority and obligation that Roman law gave to parents, and it extended over any who were in the household. It was also the metaphor that empowered those who acquired slaves. With the widespread revival of Roman law in early modern states, the hand became a feature of the slave codes adopted by the English, French, Dutch, and Spanish. Here it ceased to be only metaphorical, for these codes authorized masters to use whips, physical mutilation, or death as means of disciplining those they had enslaved. It also allowed them to grant freedom. A son, daughter, or slave who received their freedom was *e*mancipated, or set free from being under the hand of father or master. In the case of daughters, this happened at marriage, when the young woman passed from the hand of the father to that of her husband. In the case of sons it might come in the early twenties as an acknowledgment of adulthood, or only as a sign of succession on the death of the father (Kuehn 1982, 2017).

Emancipation could be potent and liberating, but it could also replace one form of exploitation with another. It relieved the one formerly in authority from any further obligations toward those whose lives had been under the controlling hand. This removed not only the rod or whip but also the hand that fed and clothed. Slaveholders in Florence, Boston, or Manila emancipated those they had enslaved when they no longer wanted the trouble or cost of providing food or shelter for them, perhaps at the point when the enslaved had grown old and were less able to work. Others did it only in their wills, waiting until their own demise before freeing their heirs from the obligation of caring for these enslaved. Amsterdam residents could not emancipate their domestic enslaved because slaveholding was illegal within the Netherlands itself. The Dutch had no qualms about buying, insuring, or selling human beings overseas, about shipping them from one side of the Atlantic to another, and indeed about relying heavily on them to work their plantations in Asia, Africa, and the Americas. Yet they refused to countenance the migration of slaves or the formerly enslaved into the Netherlands. Their ambivalence about enslavement was purely abstract and hence driven more by race and profit than by religion or morality (van den Berg 2016).

In the texts and examples handed down from the Romans, the hand symbolized authority and demanded deference. So it is interesting to see how one early modern group used the hand to symbolize its refusal to offer that deference. Quakers believed in the fundamental equality of human beings and so declined to bow, curtsy, or doff the hat to those in authority. They offered the handshake as a sign of welcome and collaboration. Asserting that the time of touch was on first meeting a stranger or friend won them no allies in early Boston, that Promised Land for the communion of the saints. We saw that Bostonians executed four Quakers for their beliefs from the late 1660s, and many others were imprisoned, beaten, and executed in mid–seventeenth-century England. Quakers adopted touch as a sign of greeting and welcome in order to demonstrate physically that they rejected artificial social hierarchies. Handshakes had long existed as a sign of peace and friendship exchanged among equals, with the added benefit of demonstrating that neither was armed or dangerous. With this meaning it appears in Assyrian reliefs, Roman coins, and medieval illuminations. The Quaker handshake was more radical than it may seem, because it asserted an equality that at least one party might find uncomfortable. The bow or curtsy was a deferential sign of greeting free of any physical contact with the social superior, while the handshake brought them down to your level (Roodenburg 1991; Muir 2005).

And from what height? Meeting the queen in London or the king in Paris, an ordinary subject was not to even look them in the eye, let alone reach for their hand. Both actions asserted familiarity if not equality. Most court societies found that unacceptable and indeed unimaginable. Royalty existed, by divine appointing and anointing, on a completely different plane than commoners. A royal hand was raised only at the sovereign's initiative, as a sign of acknowledgment or blessing. Raising the hand in touch was sufficiently rare that it was associated with miraculous healing. In this form, medieval French and English kings practiced the thaumaturgic ("miraculous") touch for scrofula, a disfiguring bacterial infection of the lymph nodes (Thomas 2005). They most commonly touched their subjects in the winter months, particularly during religious feasts. Since the infections often eased of their own accord, the monarchs' healing reputation could remain intact. Some monarchs, like Henry VIII, Elizabeth I, and France's Henri IV, used thaumaturgic touch to underscore their role in healing a broken nation – Elizabeth increased it after her excommunication in 1570, and Henri after his conversion to Catholicism brought an end to the Wars of Religion in France in 1594. England's Charles II outdid them both when his return to the throne in 1660 restored England's monarchy. He may have touched as many as 92,000, or 4,500 annually, far beyond the 1,600 that Louis XIV managed at Easter 1680 (Sturdy 1992; Lane Furdell 2001; Krieger 2002).

Thaumaturgical touch, like the healing touch of Christ, was an immediate and physical gift. It came rarely to others, like a seventh son born blind (see Figure 19). The healer had to make physical contact. What about a hand raised in blessing? Like the question of looking the monarch in the eye, this opened up a more abstract dimension to touch. Some early modern theorists of vision believed that sight was physical, believing that particles extended from the object to reach the eye and make an imprint on the brain (intromission); one variant on this theory believed that particles extended first from the eye before returning to leave their impression (extromission). This was one side of the meaning when you said that you had "apprehended" something. You'd quite literally captured it and brought it back to your own eyes and mind (Paterson 2016). These variants on visual perception become more accessible to us as we become more familiar with the ambiguities of virtual reality. That may be a way of apprehending intellectually how some signs, like a hand raised in benediction at the end of a mass by a Catholic priest in Manila or at the close of a service by a Congregational preacher in Boston, might be both purely remote and visual but also immediate, tactile, and instrumental. The ceremony of ordination bestowed on both priest and preacher the authority to conclude a Sunday worship service with a hand gesture that both used to bestow on congregants

Figure 19 The blind healer. Anon, 17th century (Wellcome Collection)

the power of God's Holy Spirit and to become agents of divine healing and blessing to others in the week ahead. That said, an early modern Italian saying held that the one who blesses knows how to curse. The inverse of the divine benediction was the witches' curse, delivered orally with or without touch.

6.2 Forbidden Touch

The royal touch might cure scrofula, but there was no such tactile healing for lepers. And while Christ's example of healing lepers by touching them was the stuff of sermons and of saints' lives, it did not shape common social practice (see Figure 20). Emerging from the Middle East and East Africa, leprosy may have been brought to Europe by returning crusaders, since we see increases in the number of institutional enclosures known as leprosaria from the thirteenth century. These enclosures were intended to keep lepers from contacting and contaminating others. While they could beg for alms, they could not move around silently but had to announce their arrival with bells or shouts. In small towns and villages on both sides of the Pyrenees, members of a group thought to be descended from lepers and known as *Cagots* or *Agotes* were for centuries forced to enter and exit churches from their own door at the side of the sanctuary so that they would not inadvertently touch others (Guerreau and Guy 1988). The random touch of a leper

Figure 20 Christ healing lepers. Leonard Gaultier, c. 1576–80 (National Gallery of Art, Washington)

was never as contagious as feared, but the debilitating disease could and would spread through close human contact. Early modern seaborne migrations, particularly the forced migrations of the enslaved on ships, carried leprosy along with many other devastating diseases to coastal West, South, and East Africa, to Central America, the Caribbean and Brazil, India, and South East Asia (Monot et al., 2005).

The touch of a diseased person might be as bad as the *mal-aria* they emitted. St Catherine of Siena famously touched the buboes of those infected with bubonic plague and even drank the pus they emitted. Yet her own immunity and healing practice were miraculous exceptions that doctors seldom imitated. Touch became a commonplace of early modern saints' lives precisely *because* these heroes of the faith defied medical wisdom when they touched the sick and dying. Doctors touched less frequently, though taking the pulse was understood as an index of heart health by the ancients even before Ibn al Nafis (1213–88) and William Harvey (1578–1657) revised classical understandings of how blood circulated in the body. Other concerns might intervene, limiting in particular the male touch of a woman. Some doctors took women's pulse from behind a curtain, and others brought midwives to carry out physical examinations of female patients, using these intermediaries' touch and explanations to assess symptoms and convey diagnoses. When midwife Caterina Schrader, working far north of Amsterdam, faced difficult births that she could not handle by reaching into the womb to physically manipulate the fetus, she called in a doctor. He took over and intervened *with art*, which is to say with tools and instruments (Marland 1987). Midwives' healing touch extended far beyond birth, as indeed that that of other female medical professionals. For the two dozen nurses in Florence's syphilitics' hospital, touch was an indispensable therapeutical tool as they cleaned, dressed, and fed hundreds of patients each year (Strocchia 2019).

Touch across gender lines was complicated enough, and a whole range of customs aimed to channel and limit it, beginning with the patriarchal hand that steered women toward early marriage and out of family inheritance. Complications multiplied when race, religion, and sex entered the equation. Catholic inquisitors condemned sexual relations of Christians with Jews or Muslims as a forbidden mixing, and Florentine officials levied stiff fines against Jews who visited Christian brothels. Rabbis reciprocated, and within Europe itself strong prohibitions absolutely forbade intermarriage. Not that there was much demand for it. The hand of household authority bent the expectations that the hand of church and state enforced rigorously. Yet while marriage across some lines of ethnicity and race was unthinkable, European heads of household and their sons and friends demanded sex from servants and the enslaved regardless of their religion or race. The offspring they generated were often abandoned to local foundling homes; half the first cohort of infants abandoned at Florence's Innocenti foundling home when it opened in 1445 were the children of enslaved mothers (Zhang 2023). Manila's Misericordia opened a home for the orphaned and abandoned children sired by Spanish merchants, sailors, and soldiers, and most of those in its *beaterios* were of similar background (Graham 2019). Amsterdam's VOC regents opened similar shelters in Cape Town and Batavia; these were often the first charitable enclosures opened by religious, state, or commercial authorities in colonial settlements (Taylor 1983; Terpstra 2023).

Over time, Europeans became increasingly anxious about this kind of sexual touch and found ways to curb or punish it. Fifteenth-century Iberian "pure blood laws" articulated difference in biological terms that would later be expressed as the "racial science" of the eighteenth century. Iberians also traced these blood lines back through multiple generations and excluded those of Jewish ancestry from some universities and religious orders, demonstrating their conviction that racialization trumped conversion (Herzog 2003). The more intensely racialized biology of the Enlightenment put an end to some forms of mixing arising out of colonialism and enslavement that had been accepted as inevitable in the preceding two centuries. French fur traders had joined Wendat and Cree families in adaptations of the adoption and inclusion that First Nations extended to wider ranges of migrants, including captives, creating in the process a distinct Metis community. Some Spanish colonists married the daughters of Aztec and Mayan aristocrats and some English officers and traders did the same with Mughal elites in India. The Dutch passed such restrictive laws on colonial mixed marriage, forbidding for instance the repatriation of Asian spouses and children to the Netherlands, that some of their colonial factors reverted to concubinage instead. The children born to colonists who married local women initially moved into positions with government administrations and monopoly trading companies as indispensable transcultural interpreters and mediators (Bosma and Raben, 2008; Onnekink and Rommelse 2019; Hämäläinen 2022). Demographic diversity and recognition varied within and between colonial cultures, yet exclusionary attitudes hardened over the course of the eighteenth century. Spanish *casta* paintings that served as virtual catalogues of the wide range of possible mixed marriages through generations categorized row upon row of abstract color-coded family portraits (see Figure 21). They lined up the tiles like a checkerboard, moving from most to least white and purporting with this to track the effect of sexual touch on color and physiognomy. The paintings showed shifting preoccupations, though we don't know whether they triggered or reflected the accelerating obsession over defining race and projecting it on others (Herzog 2003; Katzew 2005). There was no room for ambiguity in the English East India Company, where a series of orders passed in quick succession altered the lives of mixed-race families. One in three British men cohabited with Indian women, and Anglo-Indian children had frequently entered the Company's service. Yet in 1786 Anglo-Indian orphans were shut out of the Company's army, and in 1791, 1792, and 1795 further orders removed Anglo-Indian clerks from its offices and sailors and officers from its ships. After centuries as an often-subordinate collaborator with Mughal and other Indian rulers, the Company was transforming into a more overtly controlling and racially exclusive dominant power determined to remake India as its possession (Hawes 1996; Dalrymple 2019).

Figure 21 Mexican *casta* painting. Iganzio Maria Barreda, 1777 (Wikimedia Commons)

6.3 Casual Touch, Distancing Touch

Sociable touch was common at mealtimes and festivities. In homes and taverns, people met over tables and shared dishes together. Side by side, they ate directly from a common dish. If that got too messy, they might grab pieces of meat or slices of a pie from the common pot and bring it over their own plate. One

Figure 22 The thin kitchen. Pieter van der Heyden, c.1610–30 (National Gallery of Art, Washington)

reason for baking so many meats and vegetables into pies was to give them the crust that made it easier to pick up and consume by hand. Soups, stews, and the ubiquitous gruel were harder to handle, making spoons one of the standard utensils at the table. Yet here, too, you commonly reached directly into the common pot to grab your mouthful or portion (see Figure 22). Taking a drink meant reaching for a cup you shared with one or two others and hoping they hadn't left crumbs on their own last draught. Eating was tactile and communal and it was messy. As with bathing, early moderns relied on linens to preserve hygiene and propriety. Napkins and tablecloths were the necessary parts of fine dining, and to spread a cloth over a bench was to transform it into a dining table. The French traveler and writer Michele de Montaigne admitted that he seldom used either a fork or spoon but would find it uncomfortable and uncouth to eat without a napkin.

And what about those forks? Coming out of Byzantium, by the fifteenth century they were finding their way into the hands of diners in Florence, who used them for pasta, and also into frescoes, account books, and novelle. They were the leading tool in a slow remaking of the dining table and whole dining experience. Many dismissed them as overly delicate, and they did take some getting used to. They were a purely personal device, and diners wanting them had to bring their own along to a tavern or social meal. Many of the earliest ones were small, decorative, and easy to slip into a pocket, as much a way to signal your social taste as to manipulate what you tasted from the common table. A fork in the hand kept that hand from the pot. The revolution that slowly transformed mealtime over the course of the early modern period was not only one of bringing new global foods and foodways to the table and the mouth. It was a move to make the act of eating less physically tactile. And less communal, even when that eating took place in larger groups gathered around common tables and pots at a home or tavern (Grieco 2020).

The individual fork opened the way to a revolution in the act of eating. It led to individual knives, spoons, plates, and glasses. Dishes and cutlery expanded as you moved up the social scale, requiring more individual space for each diner and a complex choreographing of the placement and deployment of multiplying numbers of utensils at a table setting. Each had its designated purpose, giving it a particular size and shape. Dining tables extended their reach, and designated dining rooms replaced the multipurpose halls that had been common in the homes of the wealthy at the beginning of the period. The dining room took in the specialized furniture of fine dining: cupboards to store the cutlery and display the china and glassware, buffets and side tables to hold the plates of food that servants prepared for individual diners. It was a transformation in the space and touch of eating. Step by step, Europeans were distancing themselves from physical contact with each other and with their food. At the beginning of the period, you might reach out and grab something from the plate of someone across the table; at the end of it, this would get you thrown out of the dining room, and indeed out of polite society (Muir 2005; McIver 2015).

Part of this was commercial. While fifteenth-century tables might have a few wooden or pewter dishes, the multiplying plates, bowls, cups, and cutlery of eighteenth-century dinner services created – and were created by – new industries in pottery, glass, and metalwork. The bespoke and monogrammed designs of those at the top of the social scale found their echoes in the multiplying patterns for the popular market (see Figure 23). Excavations at the seaside home of Boston sea captain James Garrett unearthed hundreds of ceramic dishes, the bulk of them Portuguese imitations of Ming Chinese designs, which he likely picked up while trading in the Azores in the 1640s (Bagley 2021). Manila's cosmopolitan diners collected ceramics from around the Indian Ocean for their tables. Elite Europeans had prioritized expensive and delicate Chinese porcelain, and rulers invested large sums in the competitive race to produce porcelain in Europe itself. Factories in England, France, Germany, and Italy once more emulated this

Figure 23 Tea set. Jean-Étienne Liotard, 1781–3 (Getty Museum)

innovation with more affordable and robust mass-produced fine "china" to push the durable ceramic, wooden, and metal plates off the table entirely. Or at least off some tables.

Beyond the consumer drive, the revolution transforming the spaces, utensils, and tactility of dining was part of a larger revolution in manners. And that revolution focused on limiting touch. A well-mannered person did not touch their food directly at the table. In public, they did not touch themselves directly in what were now called the "private" areas of their body. We might think of the body itself as divided into zones, and two in particular. The upper body of head and torso was the body of intellect and will. The lower body of stomach and sexual organs was the body of appetite and passion. There was nothing new about efforts to have reason control passion, but translating this into a wide-ranging set of rules about how you interacted with your own individual physical body was one of the characteristic developments of the early modern period. And it didn't end with the physical body. People lower on the social scale were thought to be controlled by the passions and appetites of their lower body: they ate and drank, defecated, and had sex like animals. Once appetite hit or opportunity presented itself, they literally couldn't help themselves. The higher up the social scale you were, the greater control you exercised over your animal drives: eating at particular times and with tools, carrying out bodily needs in private, always aware of the gaze and opinion of others. No one denied that you had those drives. What marked the civilized individual was how they governed and met them, and how self-control marked their individual actions and the tastes, speech, codes, or "habitus" of their social circle (Bourdieu 1977; Elias 2000; Muir 2005).

7 Conclusion

Exploring how landscapes, soundscapes, and smellscapes came together in a sensorium gives us a more nuanced view of how early moderns imagined, constructed, and lived in the world. Sound, sight, smell, taste, and touch offered ways of telling time, shaping bodies, and directing hopes. Senses have a history and are historically constructed around distinctions of gender, class, race, and culture (Smith 2007, 2021). We can approach them almost as languages, expressed in a grammar of memories and emotions and leaving a record in customs and habits. Joined together and with space they imposed some barriers and offered ways of transcending others, as examples from Florence, Amsterdam, Boston, Manila, and beyond all demonstrate.

Focusing on sense and space gives us a distinct angle on how Europeans became steadily more obsessed with the globe through the early modern period and more impressed with their own ability to navigate and manipulate it. They were still wrestling to understand and imitate a classical Greek and Roman culture they'd inherited when new pathways out to the rest of the globe opened up. They took to these pathways in a sense of awe at cultures that were older, richer, and far more complex. Awe gave way to opportunity and eventually to a determination to assert control and to possess. We can and must understand the economics and politics of these often violent processes of capitalism, imperialism, and colonialism, particularly as they developed into the confident sense of superiority that marked Enlightenment modernity. Looking to sense and space can help us discern how Europeans aimed to legitimate a sometimes fragile domination that few elsewhere in the world conceded, however much they might be increasingly subject to Europeans' growing physical and economic control. Impressive architectural monuments, new colonial hubs anchoring global trading networks, and complex codes of diet, manners, and clothing all led Europeans to exaggerate their powers of rationality and self-control. They believed that their domination came out of personal effort and divine or historical destiny rather than as a largely chance convergence aided by strategic violence. Moreover, at home and abroad they increasingly defined what they were by using sensory markers of what they were not, and then projecting those characteristics – being dirty, smelly, noisy, slovenly – on those they dominated. This rationalized and legitimated their control over others and allowed them to assume for themselves a God-given "civilizing" mission that justified enslavement as spiritual care and saw global economic and cultural domination as both reward and obligation.

Recovering their developing soundscapes, smellscapes, and landscapes gives us the best means of mapping Europeans' expanding horizon of possibilities through a period when their sense of their own relation with the world was steadily shifting. Their classical and Christian inheritances had long shaped their experience of space and the sensorium. Their ways of navigating complex intercultural places, spaces, and relations would become more fraught as they aimed to push from dependence to domination and control. The complexities of global convergences and divergences involved a host of factors beyond the sensorium. Yet it was in the realms of sight, hearing, smell, taste, and touch, played out over far-flung spaces, that this domination became immediate, personal, and cultural.

References

Abrahamse, Jaap Evert. 2019. *Metropolis in the Making: A Planning History of Amsterdam in the Dutch Golden Age*. (Turnhout: Brepols)

Albala, Ken. 2011. "The Ideology of Fasting in the Reformation Era," in Ken Albala and Trudy Eden (eds.), *Food and Faith in Christian Culture* (New York: Columbia University Press): 41–57

Albala, Ken (ed.). 2013. *A Cultural History of Food in the Renaissance* (London: Bloomsbury)

Allen, Joanne. 2022. *Transforming the Church Interior in Renaissance Florence* (Cambridge: Cambridge University Press)

Alpers, Svetlana. 1983. *The Art of Describing: Dutch Art in the Seventeenth Century* (Chicago: University of Chicago Press)

Angeles, F. DeLor. 1980. "The Philippine Inquisition: A Survey." *Philippine Studies* 28, no. 3 (1980): 253–283

Appadurai, Arjun. 1996. *Modernity at Large: Cultural Dimensions of Globalization* (Minneapolis: University of Minnesota Press)

Atkinson, Niall. 2016. *The Noisy Renaissance: Sound, Architecture, and Florentine Urban Life* (University Park: Pennsylvania State University Press)

Attlee, Helena. 2014. *The Land Where Lemons Grow: The Story of Italy and Its Citrus Fruit* (London: Particular Books)

Bagley, Joseph M. 2021. *A History of Boston in 50 Artifacts* (Waltham, MA: Brandeis University Press)

Baldauf-Berdes, Jane J. 1996. *Women Musicians of Venice: Musical Foundations, 1525–1855* (Oxford: Oxford University Press)

Bell, Rudolph M. 1999. *How to Do It: Guides to Good Living for Renaissance Italians* (Chicago: University of Chicago Press)

Benoit, Jean-Louis. 2012. "Autour de l'odeur de sainteté, les parfums dans le monde chrétien." *IRIS* 33: 55–89

Bertoglio, Chiara. 2017. *Reforming Music: Music and the Religious Reformations of the Sixteenth Century* (Berlin: De Gruyter)

Boddice, Rob and Mark Smith. 2020. *Emotion, Sense, Experience* (Cambridge: Cambridge University Press)

Bosma, Ulbe and Rembo Raben. 2008. *Being "Dutch" in the Indies: A History of Creolisation and Empire, 1500–1920* (Singapore: National University of Singapore Press)

Bourdieu, Pierre. 1977. *Outline of a Theory of Practice* (Cambridge: Cambridge University Press)

Bowen, Joanne. 1998. "To Market, to Market: Animal Husbandry in New England Sources." *Historical Archaeology* 32, no. 3: 137–152

Brook, Tim. 2007. *Vermeer's Hat: The Seventeenth Century and the Dawn of the Global World* (London: Bloomsbury)

Brown, Christopher Boyd. 2005. *Singing the Gospel: Lutheran Hymns and the Success of the Reformation* (Cambridge, MA: Harvard University Press)

Brown, Katherine M. 2009. *Foul Bodies: Cleanliness in Early America* (New Haven, CT: Yale)

Burke, Peter. 1984. "How to Become a Counter-Reformation Saint," in Kaspar von Greyerz (ed.), *Religion and Society in Early Modern Europe, 1500–1800* (London: German Historical Institute): 45–55

Campbell, Jodi. 2017. *At the First Table: Food and Social Identity in Early Modern Spain* (Lincoln: University of Nebraska)

Cashmere, John. 1991. "The Social Uses of Violence in Ritual: Charivari or Religious Persecution?" *European History Quarterly* 21: 291–319

Cassen, Flora. 2017. *Marking the Jews in Renaissance Italy: Politics, Religion, and the Power of Symbols* (Cambridge: Cambridge University Press)

Cassen, Flora. 2018. "The Sausage in the Jews' Pantry: Food and Jewish–Christian Relations in Renaissance Italy," in Hasia Diner and Simone Cinotto (eds.), *Global Jewish Foodways, A History* (Lincoln: University of Nebraska Press): 27–49

Champion, Matthew S. 2017. *The Fullness of Time: Temporalities of the Fifteenth Century Lowlands* (Chicago: University of Chicago Press)

Cheek, Charles D. 1998. "Massachusetts Bay Foodways: Regional and Class Influences." *Historical Archaeology* 32, no. 3: 153–172

Chong, Alan. 1987. "The Market for Landscape Painting in 17th-Century Holland," in Peter Sutton (ed.), *Masters of 17th-Century Dutch Landscape Painting: Catalogue of Exhibitions Held at the Rijksmuseum, Amsterdam; Museum of Fine Arts, Boston and the Philadelphia Museum of Art* (Boston, MA: Museum of Fine Arts)

Cowan, Brian. 2011. *The Social Life of Coffee: The Emergence of the British Coffee House* (New Haven, CT: Yale University Press)

Craig, John. 2005. "Psalms, Groans and Dogwhippers: The Soundscape of Worship in the English Parish Church, 1547–1642," in Will J. Coster and Andrew Spicer (eds.), *Sacred Space in Early Modern Europe* (Cambridge: Cambridge University Press): 104–123

Crosby, Alfred W. 1972. *The Columbian Exchange: Biological and Cultural Consequences of 1492* (Westport, CT: Greenwood Press)

Dalrymple, William. 2019. *The Anarchy: The East India Company, Corporate Violence, and the Pillage of an Empire* (London: Bloomsbury)

De Certeau, Michel. 1984. *The Practice of Everyday Life* (Berkeley: University of California Press)

Dempsey, Genevieve E. V. 2018. "Healing the Middle Passage with Parade: Music and Movement in Afro-Catholic Brazil." *Transition* 125: 158–169

Dierksmeier, Laura. 2020. *Charity for and by the Poor: Franciscan and Indigenous Confraternities in Mexico, 1527–1700* (Norman: University of Oklahoma Press)

Ditchfield, Simon. 1992. "How Not to Be a Counter-Reformation Saint." *Papers of the British School at Rome* 60: 379–422

Durstler, Eric. 2012. "Food and Politics," in Ken Albala (ed.), *Cultural History of Food in the Renaissance* (London: Bloomsbury): 83–100

Eckstein, Nicholas A. 2018. "Prepositional City: Spatial Practice and Micro-neighbourhood in Renaissance Florence." *Renaissance Quarterly* 71, no. 4 (Winter): 1235–1271

Eiche, Sabine. 2004. *Presenting the Turkey: The Fabulous Story of a Flamboyant and Flavourful Bird.* (Florence: Centro Di)

Elias, Norbert. 2000. *The Civilizing Process. Sociogenetic and Psychogenetic Investigations,* rev. ed. (Oxford: Basil Blackwell)

Filippi, Daniele V. and Michael Noone (eds.). 2017. *Listening to Early Modern Catholicism: Perspectives from Musicology* (Leiden: Brill)

Finucci, Valeria. 2003. *Manly Masquerade: Masculinity, Paternity, and Castration in the Italian Renaissance* (Raleigh, NC: Duke University Press)

Fitzpatrick, Joan. 2013. "Body and Soul," in Ken Albala (ed.), *Cultural History of Food in the Renaissance* (London: Bloomsbury): 151–169

Friedenreich, David M. 2015. *Foreigners and Their Food: Constructing Otherness in Jewish, Christian, and Islamic Law* (Berkeley: University of California Press)

Friedman, David. 1988. *Florentine New Towns: Urban Design in the Late Middle Ages* (Cambridge, MA: MIT Press)

Fromont, Cécile. 2014. *The Art of Conversion: Christian Visual Culture in The Kingdom of Kongo* (Raleigh: University of North Carolina Press)

Fromont, Cécile, ed. 2019. *Afro-Catholic Festivals in the Americas: Performance, Representation, and the Making of the Black Atlantic Tradition* (University Park: Pennsylvania State University Press)

Galanaud, Anne and Pierre Galanaud. 2020. "L'entrée des Dijonnais dans la deuxième pandémie de peste." *Revue scientifique Bourgogne-Franche-Comté Nature* 31: 145–154

Geltner, Guy. 2019. *Roads to Health: Infrastructure and Urban Well-Being in Later Medieval Italy* (Philadelphia: University of Pennsylvania Press)

Gentilcore, David. 2016. *Food and Health in Early Modern Europe* (London: Bloomsbury)

Glatter, Kathryn A, and Paul Finkelman. 2021. "History of the Plague: An Ancient Pandemic for the Age of COVID-19." *The American Journal of Medicine*, 134, no. 2: 176–181

Gobin, Anuradha. 2021. *Picturing Punishment: The Spectacle and Material Afterlife of the Criminal Body in the Dutch Republic* (Toronto: University of Toronto Press)

Graham, Allison. 2019. "Maintaining Colonial Order: Institutional Enclosure in Spanish Manila, 1590–1790," in Nicholas Terpstra (ed.), *Global Reformations: Transforming Early Modern Religions, Societies, and Cultures* (London: Routledge): 134–150

Grieco, Allen J. 2020. *Food, Social Politics, and the Order of Nature in Renaissance Italy* (Florence: Villa I Tatti)

Guerreau, Alain and Yves Guy. 1988. *Les Cagots du Béarn* (Paris: Minerve)

Hämäläinen, Pekka. 2022. *Indigenous Continent: The Epic Contest for North America* (New York: Liveright)

Harrington, Joel F. 2009. *The Unwanted Child: The Fate of Foundlings, Orphans, and Juvenile Criminals in Early Modern Germany* (Chicago: University of Chicago Press)

Harvey, Elizabeth D. 2003. *Sensible Flesh: On Touch in Early Modern Culture* (Philadelphia: University of Pennsylvania Press)

Hawes, Christopher J. 1996. *Poor Relations: The Making of a Eurasian Community in British India, 1733–1833* (London: Psychology Press)

Henderson, John. 2019. *Florence under Siege: Surviving Plague in an Early Modern City* (London: Yale University Press)

Hertzberg, Arthur. 1991. *The Jews in America: Four Centuries of an Uneasy Encounter* (New York: Columbia University Press)

Herzog, Tamar. 2003. *Defining Nature: Immigrants and Citizens in Early Modern Spain and Spanish America* (New Haven, CT: Yale University Press)

Hoover, Cynthia Adams. 1985. "Epilogue to Secular Music in Massachusetts," in Barbara Lambert (ed.), *Music in Colonial Massachusetts 1630–1820, Volume II: Music in Homes and Churches* (Boston: Colonial Society of Massachusetts): 715–867

Horowitz, Elliott. 1989. "Coffee, Coffehouses, and the Nocturnal Rituals of Early Modern Jewry." *AJS Review* 14/1 (1989): 17–46.

Kabat-Zinn, Jon. 2013. "Touchscape." *Mindfulness* 4: 389–391

Kaplan, Yosef. 2000. *An Alternative Path to Modernity: The Sephardi Diaspora in Western Europe* (Leiden: Brill)

Katz, Dana E. 2017. *The Jewish Ghetto and the Visual Imagination of Early Modern Venice* (Cambridge: Cambridge University Press)

Katzew, I. 2005. *Casta Painting: Image and Race in Eighteenth Century Mexico* (New Haven, CT: Yale University Press)

Kehoe, Marsely L. 2023. *Trade, Globalization, and Dutch Art and Architecture: Interrogating Dutchness and the Golden Age* (Amsterdam: Amsterdam University Press)

Kissane, Christopher. 2018. *Food, Religion, and Communities in Early Modern Europe* (London: Bloomsbury)

Klaver, Irene J. 2014. "Dutch Landscape Painting: Documenting Globalization and Environmental Imagination," *Proceedings from the Document Academy* 1, no. 1: #12

Knighton, Tess. 2018. *Hearing the city in early modern Europe* (Turnhout: Brepols)

Koslofsky, Craig M. 2000. *The Reformation of the Dead: Death and Ritual in Early Modern Germany, 1450–1700.* (Basingstoke: Macmillan)

Krieger, Dolores. 2002. *Therapeutic Touch as Transpersonal Healing* (Woodstock, NY: Lantern Books)

Krondl, Michael. 2013. "Food Systems: Pepper, Herring, Beer," in Ken Albala (ed.), *Cultural History of Food in the Renaissance* (London: Bloomsbury): 45–62

Kuehn, Thomas. 1982. *Emancipation In Late Medieval Florence* (New Brunswick, NJ: Rutgers University Press)

Kuehn, Thomas. 2017. *Gender and Family Life in Italy, 1300–1600* (Cambridge: Cambridge University Press)

Lambert, Barbara. 1985. *Music in Colonial Massachusetts 1630–1820, Volume II: Music in Homes and Churches* (Boston: Colonial Society of Massachusetts)

Landon, David B. 1996. "Feeding Colonial Boston: A Zoo-archaeological Study." *Historical Archaeology* 30, no. 1: 1–153

Lane Furdell, Elizabeth. 2001. *The Royal Doctors, 1485–1714: Medical Personnel at the Tudor and Stuart Courts* (Rochester, NY: University of Rochester Press)

Leader, Anne. 2023. "The Family Tombs of Santa Maria degli Innocenti," in Nicholas Terpstra (ed.), *Lost and Found: Locating Foundlings in the Early Modern World* (Rome: Officina Libraria): 135–164

Lefevre, Henri. 1991. *The Production of Space.* Trans David Nicholson Smith (Oxford: Blackwell)

Le Jeune, Paul. 1635. "Relation of What Occurred in New France in the Year 1634," in Reuben G. Thwaites (ed.), *The Jesuit Relations: Volume 4 and Allied Documents: Travels and Explorations of the Jesuit Missionaries in New France, 1610–1791* (Cleveland, OH: Burrows Brothers): 89–317.

Le Maguer, Sterenn. 2015. "The Incense Trade during the Islamic Period." *Proceedings of the Seminar for Arabian Studies* 45: 175–83.

Lindborg, PerMagnus and Kongmeng Liew. 2021. "Real and Imagined Smellscapes." *Frontiers in Psychology* 12: 718172

Logue, Alexandra. 2021. "'Saucy Stink': Smells, Sanitation, and Conflict in Early Modern London." *Renaissance & Reformation/Renaissance et Reforme* 44, no. 2: 61–86

Marland, Hilary (ed.). 1987. *Mother and Child Were Saved: The Memoirs (1693–1740) of the Frisian Midwife Catharina Schrader* (Amsterdam: Editions Rodopi)

McCants, Anne E. C. 1997. *Civic Charity in a Golden Age: Orphan Care in Early Modern Amsterdam* (Urbana: University of Illinois Press)

McClive, Cathy. 2016. *Menstruation and Procreation in Early Modern France* (London: Routledge)

McIver, Katherine A. 2015. *Cooking and Eating in Renaissance Italy* (Lanham, MD: Rowman & Littlefield)

Mesquida, Juan O. 2018. "Holy Week Processions in the Philippines: A Devotional and Artistic Tradition on the Rise." *Journal of History* 64, no. 1

Mintz, Sidney. 1985. *Sweetness and Power: The Place of Sugar in Modern History* (New York: Viking)

Monot, Marc, Nadine Honoré, Thierry Garnier, et al. May 2005. "On the Origin of Leprosy". *Science* 308, no. 5724: 1040–1042

Monroe, Alicia. 2023. "Black Brotherhoods in the Portuguese Atlantic," in *Oxford Research Encyclopedia of Latin American History* (Oxford: Oxford University Press)

Montanari, Massimo. 2010. *Cheese, Pears, and History in a Proverb* (New York: Columbia University Press)

Muir, Edward. 1998. *Mad Blood Stirring: Vendetta in Renaissance Italy* (Baltimore, MD: Johns Hopkins)

Muir, Edward. 2005. *Ritual in Early Modern Europe* (2nd ed.; Cambridge: Cambridge University Press)

Newson, Linda. 2009. *Conquest and Pestilence in the Early Spanish Philippines* (Honolulu: University of Hawaii Press)

Nora, Pierre. 1989. "Between Memory and History: *Les Lieux de Mémoire.*" *Representations* 26: 18–19

Nora, Pierre, ed. 1998. *Realms of Memory: Rethinking the French Past* (Chicago: University of Chicago Press)

Onnekink, David and Gijs Rommelse. 2019. *The Dutch in the Early Modern World: A History of a Global Power* (Cambridge: Cambridge University Press)

Paterson, Mark. 2016. *Seeing with the Hands: Blindness, Vision, and Touch after Descartes* (Edinburgh: Edinburgh University Press)

Peterson, Mark. 2019. *The City State of Boston: The Rise and Fall of an Atlantic Power, 1630–1865* (Princeton, NJ: Princeton University Press)

Philips, John Edward. 1983. "African Smoking and Pipes." *The Journal of African History* 24, no. 3: 303–319

Porteous, J. Douglas. 1985. "Smellscape." *Progress in Physical Geography* 9: 356–378

Pratt, Mary Louise. 2008. *Imperial Eyes: Travel Writing and Transculturation* (2nd ed.; London: Routledge)

Prendergast, Mark. 2019. *Uncommon Grounds: The History of Coffee and How It Transformed Our World* (New York: Basic Books)

Presciutti, Diana B. 2023. "Signs of Belonging: Identifying Female Foundlings and Orphans in Early Modern Europe," in Nicholas Terpstra (ed.), *Lost and Found: Locating Foundlings in the Early Modern World* (Rome: Officina Libraria): 215–248

Pugh, Gillian. 2007. *London's Forgotten Children: Thomas Coram and the Foundling Hospital* (Stroud: The History Press)

Puttevils, Jeroen. "Invoking Fortuna and Speculating on the Future: Lotteries in the 15th and 16th Century Low Countries." *Quaderni Storici* 52, no. 3: 699–725

Raines, Francis R. 1853. *The Derby Household Books: Comprising an Account of the Household Regulations and Expenses of Edward and Henry, Third and Fourth Earls of Derby (William Ffarinton, comptroller)* (London: Chetham Society)

Read, Sarah. 2013. *Menstruation and the Female Body in Early Modern England* (London: Palgrave Macmillan)

Reed, Marcia. 2015. "Feasting in the Streets: Carnival and the *Cuccagna*," in Marcia Reed (ed.), *The Edible Monument: The Art of Food for Festivals* (Los Angeles: Getty Research Institute): 73–100

Reyes, Raquel A. G. 2017. "Flaunting It: How the Galleon Trade Made Manila, circa 1571–1800." *Early American Studies: An Interdisciplinary Journal* 15 no. 4: 683–713

Roberts, Penny. 2000. "Contesting Sacred Space: Burial Disputes in Sixteenth Century France," in Bruce Gordon an Peter Marshall, *The Place of the Dead: Death and Remembrance in Late Medieval and Early Modern Europe* (Cambridge: Cambridge University Press): 131–148

Rombough, Julia. 2024. *A Veil of Silence: Women and Sound in Renaissance Italy* (Cambridge, MA: Harvard University Press)

Roodenburg, Herman. 1991. "The 'Hand of Friendship': Shaking Hands and Other Gestures in the Dutch Republic," in Jan Bremmer and Herman Roodenburg (eds.), *A Cultural History of Gesture* (Ithaca, NY: Cornell University Press): 152–189

Rosenthal, David. 2015. *Kings of the Street: Power, Community, and Ritual in Renaissance Florence* (Turnhout: Brepols)

Rossiaud, Jacques. 1988. *Medieval Prostitution* (Oxford: Basil Blackwell)

Rubin, Miri. 2020. *Cities of Strangers: Making Lives in Medieval Europe* (Cambridge: Cambridge University Press).

Rubright, Marjorie. 2014. *Doppelgänger Dilemmas: Anglo-Dutch Relations in Early Modern English Literature and Culture* (Philadelphia: University of Pennsylvania Press)

Salzberg, Rosa. 2018. "Controlling and Documenting Migration via Urban 'Spaces of Arrival' in Early Modern Venice," in Hilde Greefs and Anne Winter (eds.), *Migration Policies and Materialities of Identification in European Cities Papers and Gates, 1500–1930s* (London: Routledge): 27–45

Schafer, R. Murray. 1977. *The Soundscape: Our Sonic Environment and the Tuning of the World* (New York: Simon and Schuster)

Schama, Simon. 1995. *Landscape and Memory* (New York: Alfred A. Knopf)

Siegmund, Stefanie B. 2006. *The Medici State and the Ghetto of Florence: The Construction of an Early Modern Jewish Community* (Stanford, CA: Stanford University Press)

Smith, Archibald W. 1997. *A Gardener's Handbook of Plant Names: Their Meanings and Origins* (Mineola, NY: Dover Publications)

Smith, Bruce R. 1999. *The Acoustic World of Early Modern England: Attending to the O-Factor* (Chicago: University of Chicago Press)

Smith, Jeffrey Chipps. 2002. *Sensuous Worship: Jesuits and the Art of the Early Catholic Reformation in Germany* (Princeton, NJ: Princeton University Press)

Smith, Mark M. 2007. *Sensing the Past: Seeing, Hearing, Smelling, Tasting, and Touching in History* (Berkeley: University of California Press)

Smith, Mark M. 2021. *A Sensory History Manifesto* (University Park: University of Pennsylvania Press)

Stevens Crawshaw, Jane L. 2016. *Plague Hospitals: Public Health for the City in Early Modern Venice* (London: Routledge)

Stow, Kenneth. 2001. *Theatre of Acculturation: The Roman Ghetto in the Sixteenth Century* (Seattle: University of Washington Press)

Stow, Kenneth. 2024. *Feeding the Eternal City: Jewish and Christian Butchers in the Roman Ghetto* (Cambridge, MA: Harvard University Press)

Strocchia, Sharon. 2019. *Forgotten Healers: Women and the Pursuit of Health in Late Renaissance Italy* (Cambridge, MA: Harvard University Press)

Sturdy, David J. 1992. *The Royal Touch in England. European Monarchy: Its Evolution and Practice from Roman Antiquity to Modern Times* (Stuttgart: Franz Steiner Verlag)

Taylor, Jane G. 1983. *The Social World of Batavia: European and Eurasian in Dutch Asia* (Madison: University of Wisconsin Press)

Tazzara, Correy. 2017. *The Free Port of Livorno and the Transformation of the Mediterranean World, 1574–1790.* (Oxford: Oxford University Press)

Teller, Adam. 2020. *Rescue the Surviving Souls: The Great Jewish Refugee Crisis of the Seventeenth Century* (Princeton, NJ: Princeton University Press)

Terpstra, Nicholas (ed). 2008. *The Art of Executing Well: Rituals of Execution in Renaissance Italy.* (Kirksville, MO: Truman State University Press)

Terpstra, Nicholas. 2013. *Cultures of Charity: Women and the Reform of Poor Relief in Renaissance Italy* (Cambridge, MA: Harvard University Press)

Terpstra, Nicholas. 2015a. "Body Politics: The Criminal Body between Public and Private." *Journal of Medieval and Early Modern Studies* 45, no. 1: 7–52

Terpstra, Nicholas. 2015b. *Religious Refugees in the Early Modern World: An Alternative History of the Reformation* (Cambridge: Cambridge University Press)

Terpstra, Nicholas. 2015c. "Sex and the Sacred: Negotiating Spatial and Sensory Boundaries in Renaissance Florence." *Radical History Review* 121: 71–90

Terpstra, Nicholas (ed). 2023. *Lost and Found: Locating Foundlings in the Early Modern World* (Rome: Officina Libraria)

Terry, Allie. 2010. "Criminal Vision in Early Modern Florence: Fra Angelico's Altarpiece for 'Il Tempio" and the Magdalenian Gaze," in John S. Hendrix and Charles H. Carman (eds.), *Renaissance Theories of Vision* (Farnham: Ashgate): 47–48.

Thomas, Keith. 2005. "Magical Healing: The King's Touch," in Constance Classen (ed.), *The Book of Touch* (Oxford: Berg): 354–362

Tolan, John V. 2005. *Sons of Ishmael: Muslims through European Eyes in the Middle Ages* (Oxford: Oxford University Press)

Torre, Angelo. 1995. *Il consume di devozioni: Religione e comunità nelle campagne dell'ancien regime* (Venice: Marsilio)

Torre, Angelo. 2019. *Production of Locality in the Early Modern and Modern Age: Places* (London: Routledge)

Trachtenberg, Marvin. 1997. *Dominion of the Eye: Urbanism, Art, and Power in Early Modern Florence* (Cambridge: Cambridge University Press)

Tremml-Werner, Birgit. 2015. *Spain, China, and Japan in Manila, 1571–1644: Local Comparisons and Global Connections* (Amsterdam: Amsterdam University Press)

Truax, Barry. 2016. "Acoustic Space, Community, and Virtual Soundscapes," in Marcel Cobussen, Vincent Meelberg, and Barry Truax (eds.), *The Routledge Companion to Sounding Art* (London: Routledge): 253–263

Valerio, Miguel A. 2020. "Black Dancers and Musicians Performing Afro-Christian Identity in Early Modern Spain and Portugal." *Palara* 24: 47–56

Valerio, Miguel A. 2022. "Black Brotherhoods in the Iberian Atlantic," in *Oxford Research Encyclopedia of Latin American History* (Oxford: Oxford University Press)

van den Berg, Peter A. J. 2016. "Slaves: Persons or Property? The Roman Law on Slavery and Its Reception in Western Europe and Its Overseas Territories." *Osaka University Law Review* 63: 171–188

Vanhaelen, Angela. 2012. *The Wake of Iconoclasm: Painting the Church in the Dutch Republic* (University Park: Pennsylvania State University Press)

Van Tielhof, Mija. 2002. *The Mother of All Trades: The Baltic Grain Trade in Amsterdam from the Late Sixteenth to the Nineteenth Century* (Leiden: Brill)

Walden, Justine. 2019. "Before the Ghetto: Spatial Logics, Jewish Experience, and Jewish-Christian relations in Early Modern Florence," in Nicholas Terpstra (ed), *Global Reformations: Transforming Early Modern Religions, Societies, and Cultures* (London: Routledge): 97–114

Ward, W. Peter. 2019. *The Clean Body: A Modern History* (Montreal: McGill-Queens University Press)

Willis, Jonathan. 2018. *Church Music and Protestantism in Post-Reformation England: Discourses, Sites and Identities* (London: Routledge)

Wisch, Barbara and Nerida Newbiggin. 2013. *Acting on Faith: The Confraternity of the Gonfalone in Renaissance Rome* (Philadelphia, PA: Saint Joseph's University Press)

Xiao, Jieling, Malcolm Tait and Jian Kang. 2018. "A Perceptual Model of Smellscape Pleasantness." *Cities* 76: 105–115

Zhang, Angela. 2023. "Hidden in Plain Sight: The Ospedale degli Innocenti and Enslavement in Fifteenth Century Florence," in Nicholas Terpstra (ed.), *Lost and Found: Locating Foundlings in the Early Modern World* (Rome: Officina Libraria): 295–314

Zolli, Daniel M. and Christopher Brown. 2019. "Bell on Trial: The Struggle for Sound after Savonarola." *Renaissance Quarterly* 72, no. 1: 54–96

The Renaissance

John Henderson

Birkbeck, University of London, and Wolfson College, University of Cambridge

John Henderson is Emeritus Professor of Italian Renaissance History at Birkbeck, University of London, and Emeritus Fellow of Wolfson College, University of Cambridge. His recent publications include *Florence Under Siege: Surviving Plague in an Early Modern City* (2019), *Plague and the City*, edited with Lukas Engelmann and Christos Lynteris (2019), and *Representing Infirmity: Diseased Bodies in Renaissance Italy*, edited with Fredrika Jacobs and Jonathan K. Nelson (2021). He is also the author of *Piety and Charity in Late Medieval Florence* (1994); *The Great Pox: The French Disease in Renaissance Europe*, with Jon Arrizabalaga and Roger French (1997); and *The Renaissance Hospital: Healing the Body and Healing the Soul* (2006). Forthcoming publications include a Cambridge Element, *Representing and Experiencing the Great Pox in Renaissance Italy* (2023).

Jonathan K. Nelson

Syracuse University Florence

Jonathan K. Nelson teaches Italian Renaissance Art at Syracuse University Florence and is a research associate at the Harvard Kennedy School. His books include *Filippino Lippi* (2004, with Patrizia Zambrano); *Leonardo e la reinvenzione della figura femminile* (2007), *Filippino Lippi* (2022), and two books co-authored with Richard J. Zeckhauser: *The Patron's Payoff: Conspicuous Commissions in Italian Renaissance Art* (2008), and *Risks in Renaissance Art: Production, Purchase, and Reception* (2024, a Cambridge Element). He co-curated museum exhibitions dedicated to Michelangelo (2002), Botticelli, and Filippino (2004), Robert Mapplethorpe (2009), and Marcello Guasti (2019), and two online exhibitions about Bernard Berenson (2012, 2015).

About the Series

Timely, concise, and authoritative, Elements in the Renaissance showcases cutting-edge scholarship by both new and established academics. Designed to introduce students, researchers, and general readers to key questions in current research, the volumes take multi-disciplinary and transnational approaches to explore the conceptual, material, and cultural frameworks that structured Renaissance experience.

Cambridge Elements ☰

The Renaissance

Printed in the United States
by Baker & Taylor Publisher Services